The Stations of the Cross in Slow Motion

By Eric and Suzan Sammons
from Sophia Institute Press:

The Jesse Tree: An Advent Devotion

Suzan Sammons

The STATIONS *of the* CROSS *in* SLOW MOTION

A DAILY DEVOTION FOR LENT

SOPHIA INSTITUTE PRESS
Manchester, New Hampshire

Sophia Institute Press
Box 5284, Manchester, NH 03108
1-800-888-9344

www.SophiaInstitute.com

Sophia Institute Press® is a registered trademark of Sophia Institute.

paperback ISBN 979-8-88911-068-2
ebook ISBN 979-8-88911-069-9

Library of Congress Control Number: 2023947634

First printing

For Dad,

who was devoted to the sufferings of Our Lord

and carried his share of them

Contents

IV. Jesus Meets His Mother: *Our Lady*

V. Simon of Cyrene Helps Jesus Carry His Cross: *Acceptance of trials*

VI. Veronica Wipes the Face of Jesus: *Image of God*

VII. Jesus Falls the Second Time: *Sin*

VIII. Jesus Meets the Women of Jerusalem: *Sorrow*

IX. Jesus Falls the Third Time: *Repentance*

X. Jesus Is Stripped of His Garments: *Poverty*

XI. Jesus Is Nailed to the Cross: *The Cross*

XII. Jesus Dies on the Cross: *It is finished*

XIII. The Body of Jesus Is Taken Down from the Cross: *Total gift*

Introduction

When I was a young Catholic-school student in the 1980s, our parish held the Stations of the Cross every Friday of Lent at precisely 2:20 p.m. School was out at 2:10, and all you had to do was walk across the parking lot and into the church. Most of us did just that.

The parish also had Stations on the Friday evenings of Lent at 7:30. More often than not, my father would ask me after dinner if I wanted to go along with him. We'd walk hand in hand the block and a half back to our church, where the children's purple Stations booklets had been replaced with the grown-up versions.

I was fascinated by St. Veronica. I imagined what it would have been like to see Our Lord on the Way, to speak a few kind words, to try to help Him just a little. The Stations of the Cross taught my young heart to love the suffering Jesus.

Picturing oneself on the road to Calvary is a practice that Catholics of all ages have always loved. In the earliest centuries of the Church, the faithful retraced Christ's steps—literally—by walking the Via Dolorosa in Jerusalem. As the Church increased her reach throughout Europe, imitations of the Via Dolorosa sprang up for those who could not journey to the Holy City. Eventually, these processions came to include images that helped the faithful meditate on the events of the Passion, as well as particular prayers and gestures such as genuflection and kneeling. Today, the Stations of the Cross are the most widely practiced Lenten devotion.

About this book

I did not set out to write a Stations of the Cross book, and in one sense, this book is *not* a Stations of the Cross book. The Stations are meant to be prayed all at once, in procession.[1]

After my husband and I published *The Jesse Tree: An Advent Devotion*, however, we heard from many families who wanted something like it for Lent. I had already been thinking about this very idea, given the lack of daily Lenten devotions for the home. Yet I was not inclined to invent something new. Better to uncover the old. That's why I chose the Stations of the Cross as the skeleton of this book and the insights of the Fathers of the Church and prayers of the saints as its flesh and blood.

What events have been more thoroughly explored, meditated on, and prayed over in the Church than those of the Passion of Our Lord? The treasury of writings of the Church Fathers and the saints has much to say. In fact, for the introduction to each Station and the closing prayers, this book draws from four versions of the Stations of the Cross, each written by a saint: St. Francis of Assisi, St. Alphonsus Liguori, St. John Henry Newman, and St. Josemaría Escrivá. (Quotations from these sources have been revised slightly for consistency in capitalization and tense and to adapt them for use as prayers.)

This book is meant to deepen the experience of the traditional Stations devotion by exploring in greater detail — and in slow motion — the mystery of each of the events that the Way of the Cross comprises. It reflects on each event for three or four days, walking the reader slowly toward Calvary.

Each Station calls to mind a theme for reflection, such as rejection, suffering, sin, or repentance. The theme of each Station is elaborated each day through Scripture passages that relate to the theme and reflections that unpack the meaning of them in the life of a Catholic.

On the day a Station is introduced, the passage is usually from the Gospel where the event is described. On other days, related Scripture

---

[1] A plenary indulgence is available for those who piously pray the Stations of the Cross. There are conditions particular to this devotion (such as praying them in procession) as well as the usual conditions for an indulgence.

passages are given to help deepen our understanding of the mystery we are contemplating. Prayers and meditations are designed to enliven the faith and devotion of adults yet are simple enough to engage children.

How to use this book

Set aside a certain time of day when the family is together to carry out your Lenten devotions. An adult, usually the father, can announce the Station and begin the opening antiphon, to which the rest of the family can respond (choose Latin or English, whichever is better for your family). Incorporate genuflection and kneeling as you deem helpful.

Scripture passages are printed right in this book for ease of use. The meditation can be read aloud, and the devotion can close with the prayer given or with another appropriate prayer. The Stabat Mater is included in the appendix of the book for those who wish to incorporate it.

You will notice that the names of saints and Church Fathers appear frequently in parentheses. Do not read these citations out loud as you present the meditation and prayers to your family. They are included only for you as an adult to know where the ideas and prayers originated.

If your family includes older children, you may wish to use the points for further reflection. These can be discussed together or even assigned as "homework."

If you miss a day, just pick up on the proper day instead of working through several days' devotions in one sitting. It is better to stick with one chapter each day than to hurry through several. If, however, you missed the day the Station was introduced—usually a Sunday or a Wednesday—you may wish to do *that* day instead of the current day.

Family devotions look different in every home. For many of us, the Jesse Tree generally begins with a fight among the children about whose turn it is to put up an ornament. That's okay. Press on through the challenges, and your efforts will bear fruit. Remember that you're giving your children a gift that will last a lifetime, just as my childhood parish did. You're showing them what it means to walk with Our Lord to Calvary.

"*If any man would come after me, let him deny himself and take up his cross and follow me*" (Matt. 16:24).

Jesus Is Condemned to Death

Rejection

ASH WEDNESDAY
The crowd demands Christ's Crucifixion

First Station: Jesus Is Condemned to Death

Antiphon

℣. *Adoramus Te, Christe,*
et benedicimus Tibi,
℟. *Quia per sanctam Crucem*
Tuam redemisti mundum.

℣. *We adore You, O Christ,*
and we praise You,
℟. *Because by Your holy Cross*
You have redeemed the world.

Jesus, the most innocent of beings, is condemned to death, yes, to the shameful death of the Cross. In order to remain a friend of Caesar, Pilate delivers Jesus into the hands of His enemies (St. Francis of Assisi).

John 19:1-6
Then Pilate took Jesus and scourged him. And the soldiers plaited a crown of thorns, and put it on his head, and arrayed him in a purple robe; they came up to him, saying, "Hail, King of the Jews!" and struck him with their hands. Pilate went out again, and said to them, "Behold, I am bringing him out to you, that you may know that I find no crime in him." So Jesus came out, wearing the crown of thorns and the purple robe. Pilate said to them, "Here is the man!" When the chief priests and the officers saw him, they cried out, "Crucify him, crucify him!"

Meditation
Today, Ash Wednesday, is one of the most well-known days of the Christian year. Why? It is not a celebration like Christmas or Easter. Stores don't decorate for Ash Wednesday, and no one gives gifts or plans a party for it.

But it's well known because, on this day, we Catholics are marked. We are marked with a cross—and not a pretty cross either: a black, ashy one, right there on our foreheads for all the world to see.

In receiving this mark, we have made a choice. We do not wish to join the crowd of people shouting, "Crucify Him!" We do not wish to throw up our hands like Pilate, feeling helpless. We will fight.

Just as soldiers bear an emblem, a mark, to show which commander they fight for, we bear the mark of our commander, Our Lord Jesus Christ. First given to us in Baptism, that invisible mark is reflected on our very foreheads today. The fight is on, and the enemy is sin.

How do we fight sin? The Church asks us to use three weapons: prayer, fasting, and almsgiving. Prayer is conversation with God. Fasting is prayer of the body. And with alms we give of ourselves to help others, especially those in need. Prayer, fasting, and almsgiving bring us closer to the heart of Our Lord, where sin has no foothold.

Jesus has been condemned, but let us follow Him wherever He goes.

Prayer

O innocent Jesus, I have sinned, and I am guilty; but that I may live, You gladly accept the unjust sentence of death. For whom, then, shall I live from now on, if not for You, my Lord? If I desire to please men, I cannot be Your servant. Let me, therefore, rather displease the whole world than not please You, O Jesus! (St. Francis of Assisi).

Gloria Patri, et Filio, et Spiritui Sancto, sicut erat in principio, et nunc, et semper, et in saecula saeculorum. Amen.	*Glory be to the Father, and to the Son, and to the Holy Spirit, as it was in the beginning, is now, and ever shall be, world without end. Amen.*

For further reflection

* How will you follow the Church's call to greater prayer, fasting, and almsgiving this Lent?

* Did Pilate think Jesus was guilty of a crime deserving death? How can you explain his actions?

THURSDAY AFTER ASH WEDNESDAY

The whole council sought false testimony against Jesus

First Station: Jesus Is Condemned to Death

Antiphon

℣. *Adoramus Te, Christe,*
et benedicimus Tibi,
℟. *Quia per sanctam Crucem*
Tuam redemisti mundum.

℣. *We adore You, O Christ,*
and we praise You,
℟. *Because by Your holy Cross*
You have redeemed the world.

Jesus is condemned to death. His death warrant is signed, and who signed it but I? . . . Those sins of mine were the voices which cried out, "Let Him be crucified" (St. John Henry Newman).

Matthew 26:57–65

Then those who had seized Jesus led him to Caiaphas the high priest, where the scribes and the elders had gathered. But Peter followed him at a distance, as far as the courtyard of the high priest, and going inside he sat with the guards to see the end. Now the chief priests and the whole council sought false testimony against Jesus that they might put him to death, but they found none, though many false witnesses came forward. At last two came forward and said, "This fellow said, 'I am able to destroy the temple of God, and to build it in three days.'" And the high priest stood up and said, "Have you no answer to make? What is it that these men testify against you?" But Jesus was silent. And the high priest said to him, "I adjure you by the living God, tell us if you are the Christ, the Son of God." Jesus said to him, "You have said so. But I tell you, hereafter you will see the Son of man seated at the right hand of Power, and coming on the clouds of heaven." Then the high priest tore his robes, and said, "He has uttered blasphemy. Why do we still need witnesses? You have now heard his blasphemy."

Meditation

The council found it very difficult to uncover any crime Jesus had committed. The only way was to find someone willing to lie, at least a little. That's why St. Matthew says the council was looking for *false* testimony (Origen).

When Jesus had spoken about the temple, He was referring to His own body and His Resurrection. "Destroy this temple," He said, "and in three days I will raise it up" (John 2:19). The witness, however, twisted His words to make it sound as if Jesus had threatened to tear down the temple building and then boasted about reconstructing it: "I am able to destroy the temple of God, and to build it in three days" (St. Jerome).

It was as Pilate said: this was a righteous man. In the final moments of His life, all Our Lord could be accused of was speaking the truth. He claimed to be equal with God! Blasphemy! No, not blasphemy. Truth (see John 5:18).

Remember this: the One we follow was rejected, tried, and condemned to death. And His only "crime" was speaking the truth. His life was one unified blaze of love in action. If we are to be rejected and condemned for what we do and say or how we live, let it be for living and loving others in truth.

Prayer

> O innocent Jesus, I have sinned, and I am guilty; but that I may live, You gladly accept the unjust sentence of death. For whom, then, shall I live from now on, if not for You, my Lord? If I desire to please men, I cannot be Your servant. Let me, therefore, rather displease the whole world than not please You, O Jesus! (St. Francis of Assisi).

| Gloria Patri, et Filio, et Spiritui Sancto, sicut erat in principio, et nunc, et semper, et in saecula saeculorum. Amen. | Glory be to the Father, and to the Son, and to the Holy Spirit, as it was in the beginning, is now, and ever shall be, world without end. Amen. |

For further reflection

  * What are one or two factors in our world today that have formed a culture that is likely to reject faithful Catholics?

  * What is the best interior response to rejection?

FRIDAY AFTER ASH WEDNESDAY

Christ's followers will be hated, for He was hated

First Station: Jesus Is Condemned to Death

Antiphon

℣. *Adoramus Te, Christe, et benedicimus Tibi,*	℣. *We adore You, O Christ, and we praise You,*
℟. *Quia per sanctam Crucem Tuam redemisti mundum.*	℟. *Because by Your holy Cross You have redeemed the world.*

Jesus Christ, after being scourged and crowned with thorns, is unjustly condemned by Pilate to die on the Cross (St. Alphonsus Liguori).

John 15:18–20

[Jesus said:] "If the world hates you, know that it has hated me before it hated you. If you were of the world, the world would love its own; but because you are not of the world, but I chose you out of the world, therefore the world hates you. Remember the word that I said to you, 'A servant is not greater than his master.' If they persecuted me, they will persecute you."

Meditation

No one wants to be hated. And no one wants to talk about hate when they talk about Jesus. Who would hate Our Lord—wasn't He a nice guy?

Well, saying that someone is "nice" usually means that he is easy to get along with because he doesn't challenge anyone. He never makes people uncomfortable. He flatters and accommodates others so he can get along with everyone.

By that definition of "nice," Jesus was no nice guy. When we get to know Him in the Gospels, we see that He is loving, firm, compassionate, challenging, committed, strong, truthful, diligent, and much more. But nice? No.

Maybe if He had been more accommodating, more people would have become His followers. He could have operated as a sort of "advertisement" for God, making obedience to God look fun, easy, and agreeable. Instead, He presented the truth directly and without compromise.

And He was hated. How few followers He gained during His life! When you read the Gospels, doesn't it seem as if He was rejected more often than He was accepted?

Yet, if Our Lord told people the truth about the Kingdom of Heaven in a loving and straightforward way, we, His servants, must do the same. When we do, what we are giving people is not just a bunch of our own ideas. It's Our Lord's truth. Far from being surprised when it's rejected—when we, like Our Lord, are condemned—be grateful for this sign that you are becoming like Him (St. John Chrysostom).

Prayer

> *O innocent Jesus, I have sinned, and I am guilty; but that I may live, You gladly accept the unjust sentence of death. For whom, then, shall I live from now on, if not for You, my Lord? If I desire to please men, I cannot be Your servant. Let me, therefore, rather displease the whole world than not please You, O Jesus!* (St. Francis of Assisi).

Gloria Patri, et Filio, et Spiritui Sancto, sicut erat in principio, et nunc, et semper, et in saecula saeculorum. Amen.	*Glory be to the Father, and to the Son, and to the Holy Spirit, as it was in the beginning, is now, and ever shall be, world without end. Amen.*

For further reflection

* How do we know that the apostles (other than Judas) took these words of Jesus to heart?

* Read about the life of St. Athanasius and think about how it relates to being hated for preaching and living the gospel.

SATURDAY AFTER ASH WEDNESDAY

The unfaithful tenants reject the vineyard owner's son

First Station: Jesus Is Condemned to Death

Antiphon

℣. *Adoramus Te, Christe,*
et benedicimus Tibi,
℟. *Quia per sanctam Crucem*
Tuam redemisti mundum.

℣. *We adore You, O Christ,*
and we praise You,
℟. *Because by Your holy Cross*
You have redeemed the world.

Jesus is all alone. Far off now are the days when the words of the Man-God brought light and hope to men's hearts, those long processions of sick people whom He healed, the triumphant acclaim of Jerusalem when the Lord arrived (St. Josemaría Escrivá).

Matthew 21:33–39

"Hear another parable. There was a householder who planted a vineyard, and set a hedge around it, and dug a wine press in it, and built a tower, and let it out to tenants, and went into another country. When the season of fruit drew near, he sent his servants to the tenants, to get his fruit; and the tenants took his servants and beat one, killed another, and stoned another. Again he sent other servants, more than the first; and they did the same to them. Afterward he sent his son to them, saying, 'They will respect my son.' But when the tenants saw the son, they said to themselves, 'This is the heir; come, let us kill him and have his inheritance.' And they took him and cast him out of the vineyard, and killed him."

Meditation

Jesus packs a lot into this story. For one thing, He's telling about how hard it was for the Chosen People to keep their covenant with God in the Old Testament. They often rejected God. But like the vineyard owner in this story, God was always patient with them. He continued to reach out to them (St. John Chrysostom).

God, the vineyard owner, has done all the work: He constructed the hedge and the tower and planted the vines. There was little for the tenants, His workers, to do, but even that little they despised.

Today, in the same way, God has done all the work. He has constructed the Church and established the sacraments through the immense graces won for us by Christ. In truth, there is little for us to do. But too often we are scornful of doing it.

And what is that little we are called to do? It is to gather the fruit of the vineyard to hand over to the Lord of the vineyard. This "fruit" is simply *obedience* (St. John Chrysostom).

When the vineyard owner's servants came to the workers to ask for the fruit—that is, their obedience—the workers were angry. Today, many people become angry when they are reminded of their responsibility to obey God's commands. They reject Our Lord in spite of all the gifts and blessings of the "vineyard" He established when His very life was poured out for us. "Crucify Him!" they call out.

When what God asks of us seems too much, remember how little it is compared with what He has done for us.

Prayer

> *O innocent Jesus, I have sinned, and I am guilty; but that I may live, You gladly accept the unjust sentence of death. For whom, then, shall I live from now on, if not for You, my Lord? If I desire to please men, I cannot be Your servant. Let me, therefore, rather displease the whole world than not please You, O Jesus! (St. Francis of Assisi).*

Gloria Patri, et Filio, et Spiritui Sancto, sicut erat in principio, et nunc, et semper, et in saecula saeculorum. Amen.	*Glory be to the Father, and to the Son, and to the Holy Spirit, as it was in the beginning, is now, and ever shall be, world without end. Amen.*

For further reflection

- When the vineyard owner sent his son to the tenants, where did they take him before killing him? How does this form a prophecy of where Christ will be crucified?

- The Church teaches that one danger of venial sin is that it can lead to mortal sin. How does this parable support that teaching?

II

Jesus Carries
His Cross

Suffering

FIRST SUNDAY OF LENT
The soldiers mock Jesus

Second Station: Jesus Carries His Cross

Antiphon

℣. *Adoramus Te, Christe,*
et benedicimus Tibi,
℟. *Quia per sanctam Crucem*
Tuam redemisti mundum.

℣. *We adore You, O Christ,*
and we praise You,
℟. *Because by Your holy Cross*
You have redeemed the world.

Consider Jesus as He walks this road with the Cross on His shoulders,
thinking of us and offering to His Father on our behalf the death He is
about to suffer (St. Alphonsus Liguori).

Matthew 27:27–31
Then the soldiers of the governor took Jesus into the praetorium, and
they gathered the whole battalion before him. And they stripped him and
put a scarlet robe upon him, and plaiting a crown of thorns they put it
on his head, and put a reed in his right hand. And kneeling before him
they mocked him, saying, "Hail, King of the Jews!" And they spat upon
him, and took the reed and struck him on the head. And when they had
mocked him, they stripped him of the robe, and put his own clothes on
him, and led him away to crucify him.

Meditation
Here at the beginning of the Way of the Cross, the soldiers seek to mock Jesus
by "pretending" He is a king. How little they understand their own actions!

As the soldiers dress Him in a scarlet robe, they do not realize they are
clothing the High Priest for the sacrifice of the New Covenant. For, on the
Cross, Christ will complete the sacrifice that He began at the Last Supper
with the words "This is my Body.... This is my Blood."

As they kneel before Him, hailing Him as a king, which they believe is a great joke, they do not know that even Pilate will describe Him as a king: "Jesus of Nazareth, King of the Jews" (John 19:19). They do not know that He truly is "King of kings and Lord of lords" (Rev. 19:16).

As they weave a crown of thorns, they do not know that each thorn is like each of our sins and that, from them, Christ will weave our very salvation, His crown of victory (St. Hilary of Poitiers). As King, He will indeed wear a crown, but it will be a diadem—a jewel-filled crown. Instead of the thorns of our sins, He will wear the precious gems of our humble, contrite hearts (see Ps. 51:17).

We see all of this with the eyes of faith. Far from being shameful, Our Lord's suffering is beautiful and full of meaning for us because we know that, by its merits, we are able to reach Heaven.

Let us see our own suffering, too, as precious. Uniting our sacrifices to Our Lord's suffering, they become jewels in the treasure chest of Our King.

Prayer

> *O my Jesus, I cannot be Your friend and follower if I refuse to carry my cross. O beloved cross, I embrace you. I joyfully accept you from the hand of my God. (St. Francis of Assisi).*

Gloria Patri, et Filio, et Spiritui Sancto, sicut erat in principio, et nunc, et semper, et in saecula saeculorum. Amen.	*Glory be to the Father, and to the Son, and to the Holy Spirit, as it was in the beginning, is now, and ever shall be, world without end. Amen.*

For further reflection

- What does Christ say to the soldiers as they mock Him? How should we respond when we are mocked for our faith in Him?

- The ancient theologian Origen remarked that hitting Christ on the head with the reed "scepter" surely did not injure Him, since a reed is hollow and light, yet this action occurs for a symbolic reason. What might this be?

MONDAY IN THE FIRST WEEK OF LENT
Jesus freely chooses to suffer and die

Second Station: Jesus Carries His Cross

Antiphon

℣. *Adoramus Te, Christe,*
et benedicimus Tibi,
℟. *Quia per sanctam Crucem*
Tuam redemisti mundum.

℣. *We adore You, O Christ,*
and we praise You,
℟. *Because by Your holy Cross*
You have redeemed the world.

A strong and heavy cross is placed upon His torn shoulders. He receives it gently and meekly, with gladness of heart even, for it is to be the salvation of mankind (St. John Henry Newman).

John 10:17–18
[Jesus said:] "For this reason the Father loves me, because I lay down my life, that I may take it again. No one takes it from me, but I lay it down of my own accord. I have power to lay it down, and I have power to take it again; this charge I have received from my Father."

Meditation
Between Our Lord's baptism in the Jordan River and His suffering on the Cross passed three years. During this time, Our Lord taught and healed the people of His land. His holiness was very evident, but still we read in the Gospels about many times when people hoped to kill Him. Yet, during the three years of His ministry, they were never successful.

Today, Christ explains why. He says that when He dies, it will be because He chooses to. For all of us, death will come without our permission. But Christ, though He is fully man, is also fully God. And so no one can force Him to die; He will choose to do so. He will willingly carry His Cross.

23

This shows us not only His power as God but also the greatness of His love. If Christ had been forced to lay down His life, it would be harder for us to see how great His love for us is, because it would seem He had no choice.

Our suffering has its roots in Original Sin or our own sins, but Our Lord's did not. Christ's suffering resulted only from His decision to suffer for love of us.

We, too, can choose suffering, as we do with our Lenten sacrifices. Let us unite all our sacrifices to Christ's on the Cross, where they can become part of His saving work.

Prayer

> *O my Jesus, I cannot be Your friend and follower if I refuse to carry my cross. O beloved cross, I embrace you. I joyfully accept you from the hand of my God* (St. Francis of Assisi).

Gloria Patri, et Filio, et Spiritui Sancto, sicut erat in principio, et nunc, et semper, et in saecula saeculorum. Amen.	*Glory be to the Father, and to the Son, and to the Holy Spirit, as it was in the beginning, is now, and ever shall be, world without end. Amen.*

For further reflection

* Is suffering a privilege or a curse?

* Find instances in the Gospels in which people sought to kill Jesus but failed to do so.

TUESDAY IN THE FIRST WEEK OF LENT

*Our sufferings are added to Christ's that the merits
of His Passion may be applied to mankind*

Second Station: Jesus Carries His Cross

Antiphon

℣. Adoramus Te, Christe,
et benedicimus Tibi,
℟. Quia per sanctam Crucem
Tuam redemisti mundum.

℣. We adore You, O Christ,
and we praise You,
℟. Because by Your holy Cross
You have redeemed the world.

*When our divine Redeemer beholds the Cross, He most willingly reaches
out to it with His bleeding arms. Embracing it, He takes it on His
bruised shoulders, and, as exhausted as He is, He carries it joyfully (St.
Francis of Assisi).*

Colossians 1:24-29
Now I rejoice in my sufferings for your sake, and in my flesh I complete
what is lacking in Christ's afflictions for the sake of his body, that is, the
church, of which I became a minister according to the divine office which
was given to me for you, to make the word of God fully known, the mystery hidden for ages and generations but now made manifest to his saints.
To them God chose to make known how great among the Gentiles are
the riches of the glory of this mystery, which is Christ in you, the hope of
glory. Him we proclaim, warning every man and teaching every man in all
wisdom, that we may present every man mature in Christ. For this I toil,
striving with all the energy which he mightily inspires within me.

Meditation
St. Paul suffered so much! He was imprisoned, beaten, flogged, stoned,
and shipwrecked. He was often hungry, thirsty, cold, and tired. Many

people hated him. And he was constantly concerned about the churches under his care.

Yet what he says in this passage may be surprising: that he completes what is lacking in Christ's suffering. We might wonder, how can Christ's suffering be "lacking" anything? Is St. Paul bragging about his work, comparing *his* pain to what Christ suffered for us?

Not in the least. Instead, he is giving Christ the credit for his work (St. John Chrysostom).

St. Paul taught that we, the Church, are Christ's body on earth. We are His "members," the parts of His body: His feet, His hands, His arms, His legs (see 1 Cor. 12:12–27). As St. Teresa of Ávila said, "Christ has no body on earth but yours. Yours are the eyes with which He looks compassionately on this world. Yours are the feet with which He walks to do good."

Therefore, if we are the parts of Christ's body, then when we do good things, it is Christ doing good things. When we suffer, it is Christ who suffers.

St. Paul says this kind of suffering makes him happy! Why? Because his suffering is proof that he is fulfilling his mission (Ambrosiaster). His mission is to preach and live the gospel of Christ. This cannot be done without suffering (St. Theodoret).

We may suffer, too, for preaching and living the gospel. But in this way, we participate in Christ's mission, becoming more and more like the One we follow. In this way, we walk with Our Lord as He carries His Cross.

Prayer

> *O my Jesus, I cannot be Your friend and follower if I refuse to carry my cross. O beloved cross, I embrace you. I joyfully accept you from the hand of my God* (St. Francis of Assisi).

Gloria Patri, et Filio, et Spiritui Sancto, sicut erat in principio, et nunc, et semper, et in saecula saeculorum. Amen.	Glory be to the Father, and to the Son, and to the Holy Spirit, as it was in the beginning, is now, and ever shall be, world without end. Amen.

For further reflection

- St. John Chrysostom said that, in this passage, St. Paul is saying, "Don't thank me." Why?

- Explain the saying "The blood of the martyrs is the seed of the Church."

III

Jesus Falls the First Time

Temptation

WEDNESDAY IN THE FIRST WEEK OF LENT
The Fall of Man

Third Station: Jesus Falls the First Time

Antiphon

℣. *Adoramus Te, Christe,*	℣. *We adore You, O Christ,*
et benedicimus Tibi,	*and we praise You,*
℟. *Quia per sanctam Crucem*	℟. *Because by Your holy Cross*
Tuam redemisti mundum.	*You have redeemed the world.*

The crowd has swollen into a multitude, and the soldiers can scarcely contain the angry, surging mob. Among them are those Jesus fed with the loaves and fishes, those He cured, those He taught by the lake and on the mountainside. A sharp pain pierces His soul, and Our Lord falls to the ground, exhausted (St. Josemaría Escrivá).

Genesis 3:1–6
Now the serpent was more subtle than any other wild creature that the Lord God had made. He said to the woman, "Did God say, 'You shall not eat of any tree of the garden'?" And the woman said to the serpent, "We may eat of the fruit of the trees of the garden; but God said, 'You shall not eat of the fruit of the tree which is in the midst of the garden, neither shall you touch it, lest you die.'" But the serpent said to the woman, "You will not die. For God knows that when you eat of it your eyes will be opened, and you will be like God, knowing good and evil." So when the woman saw that the tree was good for food, and that it was a delight to the eyes, and that the tree was to be desired to make one wise, she took of its fruit and ate; and she also gave some to her husband, and he ate.

Meditation
The first fall of Jesus on the Way of the Cross reminds us of why Christ came to earth. There was a great disaster to repair. Through the sin of

Adam and Eve—which we call "the Fall"—man had lost God's life in his soul and the right to Heaven.

Eve, and then Adam, gave in to temptation and sinned. During Lent, we examine our own lives for what causes us to do the same. While temptation itself is not a sin, avoiding temptation certainly helps us avoid sin.

We remember that God told Adam and Eve not to eat of the tree in the middle of the garden. But see, too, that God said they should not even *touch* it. Touching the fruit would not cause them to lose God's grace. But God warned them against touching it because He knew that even being near it, just thinking about it, would tempt them to *eat* it.

So what did the serpent suggest first? That Eve should merely look at the fruit (St. Ephrem the Syrian). He led her into temptation.

This is why we must always be vigilant against temptation. The Church asks us to pray Acts of Faith, Hope, and Love each day. These prayers remind us of our purpose on earth and our need for God. They keep us from imagining that we can be "like gods."

Prayer

> *O Jesus, it was not the weight of the Cross but the weight of my sins that made You suffer so much. By the merits of this first fall, deliver me from temptation and save me from falling into mortal sin* (St. Alphonsus Liguori).

Gloria Patri, et Filio, et Spiritui Sancto, sicut erat in principio, et nunc, et semper, et in saecula saeculorum. Amen.	*Glory be to the Father, and to the Son, and to the Holy Spirit, as it was in the beginning, is now, and ever shall be, world without end. Amen.*

For further reflection

* What is "the near occasion of sin," and what does the Fall of man teach us about it?

* We often think of St. Michael as the counterpart of Satan. Why does St. Irenaeus say that St. Gabriel is the counterpart of Satan?

THURSDAY IN THE FIRST WEEK OF LENT
Christ is the new Adam

Third Station: Jesus Falls the First Time

Antiphon

℣. *Adoramus Te, Christe,*
et benedicimus Tibi,
℞. *Quia per sanctam Crucem*
Tuam redemisti mundum.

℣. *We adore You, O Christ,*
and we praise You,
℞. *Because by Your holy Cross*
You have redeemed the world.

Loss of blood from the scourging and crowning with thorns has so weak-ened Jesus that He can hardly walk. As the soldiers strike Him cruelly, He falls several times under the heavy Cross (St. Alphonsus Liguori).

Romans 5:18–19
As one man's trespass led to condemnation for all men, so one man's act of righteousness leads to acquittal and life for all men. For as by one man's disobedience many were made sinners, so by one man's obedience many will be made righteous.

Meditation
Yesterday we remembered that sin came into the world through our first parents. Their actions wounded human nature. And since our nature as human beings is passed down from them, we receive it in this wounded form.

This brokenness in man means that when we are tempted, something in us really wants to sin (see Rom. 7:13–15). It is as if our human nature is sick (St. Cyril of Alexandria). Just as it is hard for us to run, sing, do math homework, or even be happy when our body is sick, it is often very difficult, with a sick human nature, to obey God when we are tempted by sin. What a sad state we are in!

Christ came to fix all this, St. Paul says.

What if, when you were sick, a doctor came and took your sickness on himself in order that his healing power could help you? Impossible, right? But in one sense, that is what Christ did for us. He took on our human nature, becoming a man like us. That means that he could "undo" the harm Adam did. Adam disobeyed, but Christ always obeyed.

The greatest example of this is Christ's sacrifice on the Cross: His most humble act of obedience to His Father. This gift to us is like a treasure chest of grace that can never run out. Through the sacraments Christ established during His life on earth, He gave us the way to gain this grace, grace that strengthens us against all temptation, lest we fall.

Prayer

> *O Jesus, it was not the weight of the Cross but the weight of my sins that made You suffer so much. By the merits of this first fall, deliver me from temptation and save me from falling into mortal sin* (St. Alphonsus Liguori).

Gloria Patri, et Filio, et Spiritui Sancto, sicut erat in principio, et nunc, et semper, et in saecula saeculorum. Amen.	*Glory be to the Father, and to the Son, and to the Holy Spirit, as it was in the beginning, is now, and ever shall be, world without end. Amen.*

For further reflection

* St. John Chrysostom said, "This present life is a kind of school, where we are under instruction by means of disease, suffering, temptations, and poverty . . . to be made fit to receive the blessings of the world to come." What does he mean?

* Before the Fall, was it as difficult for Adam and Eve to avoid sin as it is for us?

FRIDAY IN THE FIRST WEEK OF LENT
Lead us not into temptation

Third Station: Jesus Falls the First Time

Antiphon

℣. *Adoramus Te, Christe,*
et benedicimus Tibi,
℞. *Quia per sanctam Crucem*
Tuam redemisti mundum.

℣. *We adore You, O Christ,*
and we praise You,
℞. *Because by Your holy Cross*
You have redeemed the world.

Jesus sets off on the way to Calvary with His whole heart, but His limbs fail Him, and He falls (St. John Henry Newman).

Matthew 6:9–13

[Jesus said:] "Pray then like this: Our Father who art in heaven, Hallowed be thy name. Thy kingdom come, Thy will be done, on earth as it is in heaven. Give us this day our daily bread; and forgive us our debts, as we also have forgiven our debtors; and lead us not into temptation, but deliver us from evil."

Meditation

Our Lord taught us how to pray. The Our Father is so familiar to us that we may sometimes forget that the words of this prayer are Our Lord's very words.

Christ shows us here that when we pray, we should think first of God and of Heaven. Only after that should we think of our needs on earth. Heaven is more important than earth, for everything of the earth will one day pass away. But Heaven will never pass away.

What does Christ mean in teaching us to say, "Lead us not into temptation"? Certainly not that we must ask God not to lead us astray! Rather, we must ask for His help against the evil one, because Satan's dearest wish is that we fall into sin and remain there. "Lead us not into temptation" means "Do not allow us to be led by the tempter" (Tertullian).

What is the last thing this prayer asks? "Deliver us from evil," for, once we are safe from the evil one, there is nothing more to ask (St. Cyprian). We may fall into temptation, but we know that God always has the power to deliver us. No power of Hell and no man can separate us from God and His saving power (see Rom. 8:38-39).

Christ fell under the burden of the Cross He bore for our sins. When temptation or sin burdens us, let us turn to Him in prayer and in the sacrament of Confession so we may receive the grace He won for us.

Prayer

> *O Jesus, it was not the weight of the Cross but the weight of my sins that made You suffer so much. By the merits of this first fall, deliver me from temptation and save me from falling into mortal sin* (St. Alphonsus Liguori).

Gloria Patri, et Filio, et Spiritui Sancto, sicut erat in principio, et nunc, et semper, et in saecula saeculorum. Amen.	*Glory be to the Father, and to the Son, and to the Holy Spirit, as it was in the beginning, is now, and ever shall be, world without end. Amen.*

For further reflection

* St. Dominic Savio made a promise to Our Lord that he would sooner die than willingly sin. Why is sin, not death, the greatest tragedy in life?

* Consider every hour of your day (yesterday or today). What situations or events were near occasions of sin for you? How can you avoid them in the coming days?

SATURDAY IN THE FIRST WEEK OF LENT

We are always given strength to resist temptation

Third Station: Jesus Falls the First Time

Antiphon

℣. *Adoramus Te, Christe,*	℣. *We adore You, O Christ,*
et benedicimus Tibi,	*and we praise You,*
℟. *Quia per sanctam Crucem*	℟. *Because by Your holy Cross*
Tuam redemisti mundum.	*You have redeemed the world.*

Carrying the Cross, our Savior is so weakened by its heavy weight that He falls, exhausted, to the ground. The Cross is light and sweet to Him, but our sins make it so heavy and hard to carry (St. Francis of Assisi).

1 Corinthians 10:1–5

I want you to know, brethren, that our fathers were all under the cloud, and all passed through the sea, and all were baptized into Moses in the cloud and in the sea, and all ate the same supernatural food and all drank the same supernatural drink. For they drank from the supernatural Rock which followed them, and the Rock was Christ. Nevertheless with most of them God was not pleased; for they were overthrown in the wilderness.

Meditation

The Hebrew people had some tough times as they wandered in the desert. St. Paul looks back on those here, and he seems disappointed in how they handled their temptations, doesn't he?

God gave them certain gifts and protections: the cloud, which shielded them from their enemies; the sea, which drowned their enemies; food in the form of manna; and water "from the rock." Yet nearly all of the Israelites gave in to temptation, many times.

Certainly, the gifts and protections God gave them were miracles—how else could we explain water coming from a rock? But although these gifts were powerful, they were not filled with the grace of Christ's saving work, which had not yet happened (St. Ambrose).

We, on the other hand, have not just a cloud to obscure the vision of our enemies but the Holy Spirit to make us firm and perfect in our fight against them. We have not just the Red Sea to drown our enemies and lead us out of physical slavery but Baptism, to "drown" Original Sin in us and lead us to the freedom of the children of God; not just manna to eat but Jesus, the Bread of life; not just water from a rock but the living water of grace, won for us by Our Lord (St. Cyril of Jerusalem).

With all the great gifts we have been given, let us never forget to call upon Our Lord in times of temptation. We will not have the grace to resist temptation without asking for that grace from God when we need it (St. John Chrysostom).

Prayer

> *O Jesus, it was not the weight of the Cross but the weight of my sins that made You suffer so much. By the merits of this first fall, deliver me from temptation and save me from falling into mortal sin* (St. Alphonsus Liguori).

Gloria Patri, et Filio, et Spiritui Sancto, sicut erat in principio, et nunc, et semper, et in saecula saeculorum. Amen.	*Glory be to the Father, and to the Son, and to the Holy Spirit, as it was in the beginning, is now, and ever shall be, world without end. Amen.*

For further reflection

+ In the description of this station (above), why does St. Francis say that "the Cross was light and sweet" to Our Lord?

+ Think about a temptation you frequently face. How can you remember to pray as soon as you are confronted with it?

IV

Jesus Meets His Mother

Our Lady

SECOND SUNDAY OF LENT
Mary suffered through her Son

Fourth Station: Jesus Meets His Mother

Antiphon

℣. *Adoramus Te, Christe,*
et benedicimus Tibi,
℞. *Quia per sanctam Crucem*
Tuam redemisti mundum.

℣. *We adore You, O Christ,*
and we praise You,
℞. *Because by Your holy Cross*
You have redeemed the world.

Jesus rises, though wounded by His fall, and journeys on, with His Cross still on His shoulders. He is bent down, but at one place, looking up, He sees His Mother (St. John Henry Newman).

Luke 2:22, 25, 34–35

And when the time came for their purification according to the law of Moses, they brought him up to Jerusalem to present him to the Lord.... Now there was a man in Jerusalem, whose name was Simeon, and this man was righteous and devout, looking for the consolation of Israel, and the Holy Spirit was upon him.... And Simeon blessed them and said to Mary his mother, "Behold, this child is set for the fall and rising of many in Israel, and for a sign that is spoken against (and a sword will pierce through your own soul also), that thoughts out of many hearts may be revealed."

Meditation

One of the most painful things a mother can endure is to watch her child suffer. Yet, if her child must suffer, a mother wants to be near him.

So Our Lady, of course, followed the Way of the Cross. She was sure to come near enough for Christ to see her; she needed only to look into His eyes for Him to know all the love in her heart. She knew that He could

41

choose not to suffer and die, but her gaze let Him know that she did not for a moment wish Him to turn aside from His saving work.

This meeting was surely a silent one. Recall the Annunciation. Gabriel asked for Mary's acceptance of God's plan. Her reply? "Let it be to me according to your word" (Luke 1:38). Let it be: *Fiat* in Latin. This Fiat of Mary was the greatest word ever spoken by a human person. It is the central moment of all time and history.

As Jesus met Mary on the Way of the Cross, this Fiat was still ringing forth. There was no need for words, because Mary's Fiat had not been just for the moment in Nazareth. It had been for all time. It had encompassed even this present anguish.

Now Simeon's prophecy is fulfilled. A sword pierces the heart of Mary, as Christ is "a sign that is spoken against," utterly rejected, unto death. This moment tore the heart of Mary apart (St. John of Damascus).

Let us make the pierced heart of Mary our own. United with her ever-lasting Yes to the will of God, may we her children always know, love, and do His will with our whole hearts.

Prayer

> *O Jesus, by the pain You suffered in this meeting, grant me the grace of being truly devoted to Your most holy Mother (St. Alphonsus Liguori). Hand in hand with her, may I always console You, Lord, by accepting, always and in everything, the will of the Father (St. Josemaría Escrivá).*

Gloria Patri, et Filio, et Spiritui Sancto, sicut erat in principio, et nunc, et semper, et in saecula saeculorum. Amen.	*Glory be to the Father, and to the Son, and to the Holy Spirit, as it was in the beginning, is now, and ever shall be, world without end. Amen.*

For further reflection

- ♦ What do you think Mary prayed for immediately following this meeting with Our Lord?

- ♦ When and where does a sword appear in the account of the Fall in Genesis, and what does it represent? (See Gen. 3.)

MONDAY IN THE SECOND WEEK OF LENT

Our Lord gave us Our Lady as our mother

Fourth Station: Jesus Meets His Mother

Antiphon

℣. *Adoramus Te, Christe,*
et benedicimus Tibi,
℟. *Quia per sanctam Crucem*
Tuam redemisti mundum.

℣. *We adore You, O Christ,*
and we praise You,
℟. *Because by Your holy Cross*
You have redeemed the world.

With immense love, Mary looks at Jesus, and Jesus at His Mother. Each heart pours into the other its own deep sorrow. Mary's soul is steeped in bitter grief, the grief of Jesus Christ (St. Josemaría Escrivá).

John 19:25–27

Standing by the Cross of Jesus were his mother, and his mother's sister, Mary the wife of Clopas, and Mary Magdalene. When Jesus saw his mother, and the disciple whom he loved standing near, he said to his mother, "Woman, behold, your son!" Then he said to the disciple, "Behold, your mother!" And from that hour the disciple took her to his own home.

Meditation

One of the most important things Our Lord did on earth was to found the Church. He established the sacraments and chose the apostles, who would be the first priests. But in His final moments on the Cross, what does He say to the only one of those apostles who was there with Him? Does He give Him some final tips on running the Church? Does He tell Him to write down a Gospel?

No. He tells John that Mary is now his mother.

Again, does He thank Mary for raising Him? Does He explain anything to her about how to spend the rest of her life? Only one thing: John is her son.

Not "Treat John like your son" or even "John is another son for you." He said, "Behold, your son," so He is saying, "This now is Jesus" (Origen). St. Paul understood what Jesus meant: Paul talked about the Christian as one who can say, "It is no longer I who live but Christ lives in me" (Gal. 2:20). In whomever Christ lives, there is the son of Mary (Origen).

From the Cross, Christ gives us Mary. And He does so by telling us we are now "other Christs" or "little Christs." Christ lives in us. Let us give Him freedom to act by shaking off the chains of sin, and let us begin by loving Our Lady as He did.

Prayer

> *O Jesus, by the pain You suffered in this meeting, grant me the grace of being truly devoted to Your most holy Mother (St. Alphonsus Liguori). Hand in hand with her, may I always console You, Lord, by accepting, always and in everything, the will of the Father (St. Josemaría Escrivá).*

Gloria Patri, et Filio, et Spiritui Sancto, sicut erat in principio, et nunc, et semper, et in saecula saeculorum. Amen.	*Glory be to the Father, and to the Son, and to the Holy Spirit, as it was in the beginning, is now, and ever shall be, world without end. Amen.*

For further reflection

* The Litany of Loreto calls Our Lady the "Refuge of Sinners." Why?

* St. John Vianney once asked a devout old farmer what he did during all the time he spent gazing at the tabernacle. The man replied, "Nothing. I look at Him, and He looks at me." Why is this perhaps a more appropriate response to Our Lord's presence than a flood of words?

TUESDAY IN THE SECOND WEEK OF LENT
Our Lady leads us to Jesus

Fourth Station: Jesus Meets His Mother

Antiphon

℣. *Adoramus Te, Christe,*
et benedicimus Tibi,
℟. *Quia per sanctam Crucem*
Tuam redemisti mundum.

℣. *We adore You, O Christ,*
and we praise You,
℟. *Because by Your holy Cross*
You have redeemed the world.

The Son meets His Mother on His way to Calvary. They gaze at each other, and their looks become as so many arrows to wound those hearts that love each other so tenderly (St. Alphonsus Liguori).

John 2:1–5

On the third day there was a marriage at Cana in Galilee, and the mother of Jesus was there; Jesus also was invited to the marriage, with his disciples. When the wine failed, the mother of Jesus said to him, "They have no wine." And Jesus said to her, "O woman, what have you to do with me? My hour has not yet come." His mother said to the servants, "Do whatever he tells you."

Meditation

John's account of the wedding at Cana ends with Our Lord performing His first public miracle, a miracle that provides more wine for the wedding feast. What's going on here? Did John use precious lines of his Gospel just to show us a time when Jesus changed His mind?

No, there's much more to this event than that. For one thing, Jesus is pointing out His nature as God and as man.

His nature as man comes from Mary. And now Mary asks Him for a miracle—which must come from His nature as God. This is why He says to her, "Woman, what have you to do with me?" (St. Augustine). This word

Woman reminds us of Mary's connection to Eve. It reminds us that Jesus is Mary's Creator, as He is the Creator of all men. He is God. So He is saying, in effect, "Miracles are my department, you know" (St. Augustine).

She did know, ever since she, as a virgin, conceived her son.

He tells her that His "hour"—the time of His saving work—has not come. But then, Our Lord is not limited by time. The Lord of the universe is outside time. He is not the servant of time but its Lord.

We can again imagine a gaze passing between Our Lady and Our Lord. There was no more need for words or explanations. She immediately instructed the servants to obey Him.

This need not have happened. Christ could have begun His ministry here or another time, with no input at all from His Mother (St. Augustine). But He chose this beginning. He chose to show us Mary's faith, understanding, and power of intercession. And He gave us her only command, "Do whatever he tells you." Yes, let's do.

Prayer

> *O Jesus, by the pain You suffered in this meeting, grant me the grace of being truly devoted to Your most holy Mother* (St. Alphonsus Liguori). *Hand in hand with her, may I always console You, Lord, by accepting, always and in everything, the will of the Father* (St. Josemaría Escrivá).

Gloria Patri, et Filio, et Spiritui Sancto, sicut erat in principio, et nunc, et semper, et in saecula saeculorum. Amen.	*Glory be to the Father, and to the Son, and to the Holy Spirit, as it was in the beginning, is now, and ever shall be, world without end. Amen.*

For further reflection

* Find in the Gospels every recorded quotation of Our Lady.

* Usually Christ's "hour" is interpreted as His Passion and death. But here He indicates that His public life will also be part of the suffering of His life's mission. Why?

V

Simon of Cyrene Helps Jesus Carry His Cross

Acceptance of trials

WEDNESDAY IN THE SECOND WEEK OF LENT

Simon is pressed into service

Fifth Station: Simon of Cyrene Helps Jesus Carry His Cross

Antiphon

℣. *Adoramus Te, Christe,* *et benedicimus Tibi,* ℟. *Quia per sanctam Crucem* *Tuam redemisti mundum.*	℣. *We adore You, O Christ,* *and we praise You,* ℟. *Because by Your holy Cross* *You have redeemed the world.*

Jesus is weak and weary, on the point of death with each step. The soldiers wish Him to die not on the way but on the shameful Cross, so they force Simon of Cyrene to help Him bear His burden (St. Alphonsus Liguori).

Matthew 27:32

As they were marching out, they came upon a man of Cyrene, Simon by name; this man they compelled to carry his cross.

Meditation

What do we know of Simon of Cyrene? Perhaps he had no interest at all in the man dragging His Cross to Golgotha. Perhaps he was just trying to get around the confusion and go on his way. But the soldiers noticed him. He probably looked strong and healthy—just the type of man they needed to bear the weight of the Cross for a while so that their "guilty" man would not die on the way.

Simon had no choice. He could not disobey the soldiers without being severely punished. Yet he did choose how to respond in his heart. Once he looked on the suffering of Jesus—once he really looked—did his heart reject what he saw and feel ashamed? Or did love stir within him? Did he accept, out of human kindness, what he was called to do by the soldiers?

51

Like Simon of Cyrene, we normally don't choose the suffering that comes to us. We do not choose our share in the Cross. Sickness, loss, sadness, and confusion come to us like so many soldiers along the way, tapping us on the shoulder and saying, "Here, this is your burden now."

Though we don't choose the suffering, we choose our response, just like Simon—but with greater knowledge and grace. Simon could not have known that the shameful burden he carried was actually a trophy of victory (Chromatius). He bore it, perhaps, out of compassion for a suffering man. We, too, can bear suffering with compassion for others who suffer, but we also know, unlike Simon, that we trudge along to a place where tears are no more. Thanks to Our Lord, every trial can become a triumph.

Prayer

> *O Jesus, whoever does not take up his cross and follow You is not worthy of You. Behold, I cheerfully join You on the Way of the Cross. I want to carry my cross patiently until death, that I may prove worthy of You* (St. Francis of Assisi).

Gloria Patri, et Filio, et Spiritui Sancto, sicut erat in principio, et nunc, et semper, et in saecula saeculorum. Amen.	*Glory be to the Father, and to the Son, and to the Holy Spirit, as it was in the beginning, is now, and ever shall be, world without end. Amen.*

For further reflection

* The Fathers of the Church concluded that Simon of Cyrene became a Christian, based on Mark 15:21 and Romans 16:13. Why is this reasonable in light of Simon's experience on the Way of the Cross?

* Christ willed every aspect of His Passion, even the part Simon of Cyrene played. What was Our Lord showing us through the actions of Simon?

THURSDAY IN THE SECOND WEEK OF LENT
Loving God's will

Fifth Station: Simon of Cyrene Helps Jesus Carry His Cross

Antiphon

℣. *Adoramus Te, Christe,*
et benedicimus Tibi,
℟. *Quia per sanctam Crucem*
Tuam redemisti mundum.

℣. *We adore You, O Christ,*
and we praise You,
℟. *Because by Your holy Cross*
You have redeemed the world.

At length, Christ's strength fails utterly, and the soldiers stand perplexed. How is He to get to Calvary? They see a stranger who seems strong and active—Simon of Cyrene. They compel him to carry the Cross with Jesus, and Simon's heart is pierced at the sight of Him (St. John Henry Newman).

Luke 22:39–46
And [Jesus] came out, and went, as was his custom, to the Mount of Olives; and the disciples followed him. And when he came to the place he said to them, "Pray that you may not enter into temptation." And he withdrew from them about a stone's throw, and knelt down and prayed, "Father, if thou art willing, remove this cup from me; nevertheless not my will, but thine, be done." And there appeared to him an angel from heaven, strengthening him. And being in an agony he prayed more earnestly; and his sweat became like great drops of blood falling down upon the ground. And when he rose from prayer, he came to the disciples and found them sleeping for sorrow, and he said to them, "Why do you sleep? Rise and pray that you may not enter into temptation."

Meditation
"How many natures has Jesus Christ?" we are asked in the *Baltimore Catechism*. Even the youngest child can learn the answer: Our Lord has two

natures, the nature of God and the nature of man. He is both fully God and fully man.

If we look closely, we see this truth in Gethsemane. We even hear Jesus speak of it. His words "not my will, but thine, be done" reveal that, as a man, He did not want suffering—just like us! But these words also show that, as God, He shares fully the will of the Father.

A well-trained dog follows his master, attentive to every slight movement and every word, so that he can carry out his master's will immediately. He has his own desires—look, a squirrel!—but his master's come first. In a similar way, Our Lord's desires as a man always follow after His desires as God, desires He shares with the Father and the Holy Spirit (St. John of Damascus).

We must seek this unity of our wills with God's. We want to make our wills the servants of His, like that good dog willing to forgo the thrill of the squirrel for the higher good—obedience to his lord.

When difficulties come, pray: "Not my will, but thine, be done." Know that God works all things to the good of those who love Him (see Rom. 8:28). Yes, even tornados, even a failed math test, even a cast on your arm in the very beginning of summer. All things. But pray: it was because, in the garden, the apostles slept instead of praying that they became so tempted to abandon Christ on the Way of the Cross (Tertullian). Instead of abandoning Him for our own desires, we want to walk with Him, as Simon did.

Prayer

> *O Jesus, whoever does not take up his cross and follow You is not worthy of You. Behold, I cheerfully join You on the Way of the Cross. I want to carry my cross patiently until death, that I may prove worthy of You* (St. Francis of Assisi).

Gloria Patri, et Filio, et Spiritui Sancto, sicut erat in principio, et nunc, et semper, et in saecula saeculorum. Amen.	*Glory be to the Father, and to the Son, and to the Holy Spirit, as it was in the beginning, is now, and ever shall be, world without end. Amen.*

For further reflection

* As we work to accept the trials that we encounter in this life, Our Lord in the garden of Gethsemane is our model. Did He accept the suffering of the Cross because He wanted suffering for suffering's sake?

* Think about people you know who, through what they suffer, seem to carry a large share of Christ's Cross. How can you help and support them?

FRIDAY IN THE SECOND WEEK OF LENT

By carrying the Cross, Simon participated in its triumph

Fifth Station: Simon of Cyrene Helps Jesus Carry His Cross

Antiphon

℣. *Adoramus Te, Christe,*
et benedicimus Tibi,
℟. *Quia per sanctam Crucem*
Tuam redemisti mundum.

℣. *We adore You, O Christ,*
and we praise You,
℟. *Because by Your holy Cross*
You have redeemed the world.

Jesus is exhausted. His footsteps become more and more unsteady, and the soldiers are in a hurry to be finished. They take hold of a man who is coming in from a farm, a man called Simon of Cyrene, and they force him to carry the Cross (St. Josemaría Escrivá).

Romans 8:12–17

So then, brethren, we are debtors, not to the flesh, to live according to the flesh — for if you live according to the flesh you will die, but if by the Spirit you put to death the deeds of the body you will live. For all who are led by the Spirit of God are sons of God. For you did not receive the spirit of slavery to fall back into fear, but you have received the spirit of sonship. When we cry, "Abba! Father!" it is the Spirit himself bearing witness with our spirit that we are children of God, and if children, then heirs, heirs of God and fellow heirs with Christ, provided we suffer with him in order that we may also be glorified with him.

Meditation

St. Paul says we are children of God and fellow heirs with Jesus Christ. What does it mean to be an heir? If you are an heir of your father, it means that he plans to give you what he owns. On earth, someone's heir might receive a house, a business, or a farm.

But St. Paul says we are heirs of our Father in Heaven. So what will we receive? We will receive what our "fellow heir" receives. A fellow heir is a sibling—in this case, a Brother: Jesus Christ! What does He receive? Eternal glory in Heaven. Amazing!

Now, sometimes there are rules about inheriting things. Let's say your dad wants you to inherit his business. He could say, for instance, "You will inherit my business as long as you promise not to sell it to someone else." Well, St. Paul says our inheritance from God has a rule too. He says we will receive glory and eternal happiness, just like Jesus, "provided we suffer with him." We have the same "rules" as Jesus because He is our Brother.

Christ suffered for preaching and living the gospel (Diodorus). And this rule is part of our inheritance as His brothers and sisters. We will preach and live the gospel, and this will sometimes bring us suffering. We will have a share in the Cross, as Simon did. But the Way of the Cross is also the way to Heaven. There, we will receive our true inheritance as sons and daughters of our Father.

Prayer

> *O Jesus, whoever does not take up his cross and follow You is not worthy of You. Behold, I cheerfully join You on the Way of the Cross. I want to carry my cross patiently until death, that I may prove worthy of You* (St. Francis of Assisi).

Gloria Patri, et Filio, et Spiritui Sancto, sicut erat in principio, et nunc, et semper, et in saecula saeculorum. Amen.	*Glory be to the Father, and to the Son, and to the Holy Spirit, as it was in the beginning, is now, and ever shall be, world without end. Amen.*

For further reflection

* We say that in Baptism, we have died with Christ. How does this relate to our share in the Cross?

* St. Paul charges us to unite our sufferings with those of Christ. How, practically, do we do that?

SATURDAY IN THE SECOND WEEK OF LENT
The prayers of all the saints

Fifth Station: Simon of Cyrene Helps Jesus Carry His Cross

Antiphon

℣. *Adoramus Te, Christe,*
et benedicimus Tibi,
℟. *Quia per sanctam Crucem*
Tuam redemisti mundum.

℣. *We adore You, O Christ,*
and we praise You,
℟. *Because by Your holy Cross*
You have redeemed the world.

Simon of Cyrene is forced to help our exhausted Savior carry His Cross. If only Simon had offered his services of his own accord. But he is not invited by Christ, as you are (St. Francis of Assisi).

Revelation 8:2–4
I saw the seven angels who stand before God, and seven trumpets were given to them. And another angel came and stood at the altar with a golden censer; and he was given much incense to mingle with the prayers of all the saints upon the golden altar before the throne; and the smoke of the incense rose with the prayers of the saints from the hand of the angel before God.

Meditation
Immediately following the Station in which Our Lord meets Mary, whose heart has been pierced by the sword of her Son's suffering, Simon is recruited to help Jesus carry His Cross. Next, we will see Veronica approaching Our Lord with a gesture of mercy.

If you know what mothers are like, you know they want to help their children. And if it is not in their own power to give the help needed, they'll find someone who can.

It is no coincidence that after Our Lord meets His Mother, help comes to Him, first in the physical assistance of Simon, then in the compassion of Veronica (St. John Henry Newman). What would be a mother's first instinct after meeting her suffering son in an ordeal taxing him beyond all bearing? That mother would pray for help. And this Mother, our Mother, is a powerful intercessor.

There will be times when God calls you to hard things. You might wish He'd called someone else. But like Simon, you can't give your job to another: it's yours. Think about this: maybe by doing your part to bear Christ's Cross, you're an answer to someone's prayers. Simon was an answer to Mary's prayers for her Son, even though he could not have known it (St. John Henry Newman). Maybe you, too, are the answer to someone's prayers—even in hard times.

And the prayers you yourself offer to God for others—a sick friend, a lonely grandparent, or the grouchy cashier at the grocery store—all those prayers rise up to our Lord like incense, as St. John describes in today's passage. Be a Simon to others, and, like Mary, pray for Simons to come into the lives of all those who need help right now.

Prayer

> O Jesus, whoever does not take up his cross and follow You is not worthy of You. Behold, I cheerfully join You on the Way of the Cross. I want to carry my cross patiently until death, that I may prove worthy of You (St. Francis of Assisi).

Gloria Patri, et Filio, et Spiritui Sancto, sicut erat in principio, et nunc, et semper, et in saecula saeculorum. Amen.	Glory be to the Father, and to the Son, and to the Holy Spirit, as it was in the beginning, is now, and ever shall be, world without end. Amen.

For further reflection

+ Think about a time you may have been a "Simon" to someone who was suffering, and thank Our Lord for that grace.

+ Find out about a country where it is illegal to practice the Catholic Faith. Pray a Rosary for those who are suffering and persecuted there.

VI

Veronica Wipes
the Face of Jesus

Image of God

THE THIRD SUNDAY OF LENT
Created in His image

Sixth Station: Veronica Wipes the Face of Jesus

Antiphon

℣. *Adoramus Te, Christe,*
et benedicimus Tibi,
℟. *Quia per sanctam Crucem*
Tuam redemisti mundum.

℣. *We adore You, O Christ,*
and we praise You,
℟. *Because by Your holy Cross*
You have redeemed the world.

As Jesus toils up the hill, covered with the sweat of death, a woman
makes her way through the crowd and wipes His face with her veil. As
a reward of her piety, the cloth retains the impression of His sacred face
(St. John Henry Newman).

Genesis 1:26–27
Then God said, "Let us make man in our image, after our likeness; and let
them have dominion over the fish of the sea, and over the birds of the air,
and over the cattle, and over all the earth, and over every creeping thing
that creeps upon the earth." So God created man in his own image, in the
image of God he created him; male and female he created them.

Meditation
This passage from Genesis reminds us of God's intentional creation of
man and woman as particular expressions of who He is. In the Fifth Station of the Cross, we met the man who helped Jesus, and now we meet
the woman.

Men and women, though they have many burdens in common, often
bear their share of the Cross in different ways. At the Fall, men were warned
that now they must rely on their physical strength to sustain their lives.

They would work, in some way—and work would now be a burden. But every burden can also be a means of salvation.

Simon's service to Our Lord is a model for all Christians, but it is particularly suited to men. Simon steps in with his quiet strength and does his share of the work. Because he is an image of God, His act becomes a message of manly love.

Women were cursed at the Fall with pain in childbearing. We think of this first as physical pain, but we know, too, that mothers endure a particular kind of pain because of their capacity for love and compassion. One who loves deeply is also deeply vulnerable.

Veronica's motherly service to Our Lord is a model uniquely suited to women. Imagine the angry crowd, the abusive soldiers, and the volatile situation on the path to Calvary. Yet someone is suffering, and from that fact—not from any physical strength she possesses—Veronica takes courage. It is love, not self-confidence, that makes her brave. Blinking away her tears of compassion, she offers a clean cloth to a suffering face.

In Veronica we see the particularly feminine power to be quietly present in a difficult situation and to simply, graciously lend a hand.

Prayer

> *O Jesus, what shall I give You in return for all You give to me? Behold, I consecrate myself entirely to Your service. I give You my whole heart; stamp on it Your holy image, that I may never forget You* (St. Francis of Assisi).

Gloria Patri, et Filio, et Spiritui Sancto, sicut erat in principio, et nunc, et semper, et in saecula saeculorum. Amen.	*Glory be to the Father, and to the Son, and to the Holy Spirit, as it was in the beginning, is now, and ever shall be, world without end. Amen.*

For further reflection

- The big problems of life on earth can seem overwhelming. How can I possibly fix poverty or injustice or tyranny? How does Veronica's act help us understand what we can do to alleviate the sufferings of others?

- What women do you know who serve others as Veronica served Jesus—quietly aiding those who need help?

MONDAY IN THE THIRD WEEK OF LENT
The Word was made flesh

Sixth Station: Veronica Wipes the Face of Jesus

Antiphon

℣. *Adoramus Te, Christe,*	℣. *We adore You, O Christ,*
et benedicimus Tibi,	*and we praise You,*
℟. *Quia per sanctam Crucem*	℟. *Because by Your holy Cross*
Tuam redemisti mundum.	*You have redeemed the world.*

Seeing Jesus in such distress, His face bathed in sweat and blood, the holy woman Veronica presents Him with her veil. Jesus wipes His face and leaves upon the cloth its sacred image (St. Alphonsus Liguori).

John 1:1–4, 9–11, 14
In the beginning was the Word, and the Word was with God, and the Word was God. He was in the beginning with God; all things were made through him, and without him was not anything made that was made. In him was life, and the life was the light of men.... The true light that enlightens every man was coming into the world. He was in the world, and the world was made through him, yet the world knew him not. He came to his own home, and his own people received him not.... And the Word became flesh and dwelt among us, full of grace and truth; we have beheld his glory, glory as of the only Son from the Father.

Meditation
The Son of God came into the world to save us and for no other reason (St. Bede). He came to teach us about the true God, because without this understanding—which only He could fully give—no one could come to Him (St. Bede).

So His purpose in the world—to save us—is linked totally with the fact that He became man, a mystery that is called the Incarnation. He walked the earth; He ate and drank; He embraced those He loved. He had a face.

In the garden, Adam and Eve dwelt with God. They were not separated from Him until they sinned. Because of the Incarnation, God again "dwelt among us." Now sin would lose its sure power to separate man from God forever. Christ would provide the means to conquer sin through His death on the Cross.

Veronica's act is a powerful reminder of our God made man, our God who has a face. He endured every kind of human suffering out of love for us, to baptize our very nature with His holiness. And He still walks among us today, in two ways. He is present with us in the sacraments, to heal, to teach, to sanctify us, just as He healed, taught, and sanctified the people of His time. And He walks among us—in us. We are each His image. Let us live like the Christians, the "little Christs" we call ourselves, bringing His healing, His teaching, and His power to save into a world that badly needs Him.

Prayer

> *O Jesus, what shall I give You in return for all You give to me? Behold, I consecrate myself entirely to Your service. I give You my whole heart; stamp on it Your holy image, that I may never forget You* (St. Francis of Assisi).

Gloria Patri, et Filio, et Spiritui Sancto, sicut erat in principio, et nunc, et semper, et in saecula saeculorum. Amen.	*Glory be to the Father, and to the Son, and to the Holy Spirit, as it was in the beginning, is now, and ever shall be, world without end. Amen.*

For further reflection

- The devotion to the Holy Face of Jesus was approved by Pope Pius IX in 1949. One hundred years earlier, Our Lord had appeared to a French nun, saying, "I seek Veronicas to wipe and venerate My Divine Face, which has but few adorers!" Find out more about the history of this devotion and the Litany of the Holy Face of Jesus.

- Meditate on the face of Jesus, particularly the way in which the Crown of Thorns would have disfigured it with His Precious Blood.

TUESDAY IN THE THIRD WEEK OF LENT
The face of Christ

Sixth Station: Veronica Wipes the Face of Jesus

Antiphon

℣. *Adoramus Te, Christe,* *et benedicimus Tibi,* ℟. *Quia per sanctam Crucem* *Tuam redemisti mundum.*	℣. *We adore You, O Christ,* *and we praise You,* ℟. *Because by Your holy Cross* *You have redeemed the world.*

Moved by compassion, Veronica presents her veil to Jesus, to wipe His disfigured face. He imprints on it His holy face and returns it to her as a recompense (St. Francis of Assisi).

2 Corinthians 4:3–6
Even if our gospel is veiled, it is veiled only to those who are perishing. In their case the god of this world has blinded the minds of the unbelievers, to keep them from seeing the light of the gospel of the glory of Christ, who is the likeness of God. For what we preach is not ourselves, but Jesus Christ as Lord, with ourselves as your servants for Jesus' sake. For it is the God who said, "Let light shine out of darkness," who has shone in our hearts to give the light of the knowledge of the glory of God in the face of Christ.

Meditation
How did the Chosen People of the Old Testament understand "the face of God"? For one thing, it was to be greatly feared. Anyone who looked on it would surely die. It was understood that a sinful man could never see such a holy sight and live.

How Our Lord turned this idea on its head! He came as a man anyone could look upon, to redeem and save all men. Yet St. Paul tells us here that, for many, the good news of his work is "veiled"—hidden from their sight. Why?

It is unbelief—the refusal to have faith—that darkens the eyes of the soul (Ambrosiaster). St. Matthew reports that when Christ preached in Nazareth, He could not do many miracles because the people lacked faith. This doesn't mean Christ did not have the power to do miracles there; He is all-powerful. It means that He refuses to force people to believe in Him. He awaits our willingness to believe. Our faith lifts the veil of unbelief.

Veronica could see clearly who Christ was because of her faith. The "light of the knowledge of the glory of God" already shone within her when, removing her veil, she reached out to Him in compassion. The result of her faith? A miracle.

Prayer

> O Jesus, what shall I give You in return for all You give to me? Behold,
> I consecrate myself entirely to Your service. I give You my whole heart;
> stamp on it Your holy image, that I may never forget You (St. Francis
> of Assisi).

Gloria Patri, et Filio, et Spiritui Sancto, sicut erat in principio, et nunc, et semper, et in saecula saeculorum. Amen.	Glory be to the Father, and to the Son, and to the Holy Spirit, as it was in the beginning, is now, and ever shall be, world without end. Amen.

For further reflection

* St. John Chrysostom said that only in this world are there unbelievers. Why?

* Meditate on an image of the veil of St. Veronica, which is enshrined in St. Peter's Basilica in Rome, or on sacred art depicting Veronica and her veil.

VII

Jesus Falls the Second Time

Sin

WEDNESDAY IN THE THIRD WEEK OF LENT
Gazing at the serpent that was raised up

Seventh Station: Jesus Falls the Second Time

Antiphon

℣. *Adoramus Te, Christe,*
et benedicimus Tibi,
℟. *Quia per sanctam Crucem*
Tuam redemisti mundum.

℣. *We adore You, O Christ,*
and we praise You,
℟. *Because by Your holy Cross*
You have redeemed the world.

Outside the walls of the city, the body of Jesus again gives way through weakness, and He falls a second time, amid the shouts of the crowd and the rough handling of the soldiers (St. Josemaría Escrivá).

Numbers 21:4–9

From Mount Hor they set out by the way to the Red Sea, to go around the land of Edom; and the people became impatient on the way. And the people spoke against God and against Moses, "Why have you brought us up out of Egypt to die in the wilderness? For there is no food and no water, and we loathe this worthless food." Then the Lord sent fiery serpents among the people, and they bit the people, so that many people of Israel died. And the people came to Moses, and said, "We have sinned, for we have spoken against the Lord and against you; pray to the Lord, that he take away the serpents from us." So Moses prayed for the people. And the Lord said to Moses, "Make a fiery serpent, and set it on a pole; and every one who is bitten, when he sees it, shall live." So Moses made a bronze serpent, and set it on a pole; and if a serpent bit any man, he would look at the bronze serpent and live.

Meditation

When Christ falls again on the Way of the Cross, we remember the sorrow brought on by sin. When we sin, we have "fallen." Instead of remaining close to Our Lord, who is on high, we have been brought low.

We've considered before how, during their time in the desert, the Israelites sinned. In today's passage, we see their impatience and their constant complaining. Their hearts were turned against God, even though He had saved them from the Egyptians! It wasn't until the poisonous serpents showed up that they realized how far they had fallen away from God. Then they begged for help.

To be saved, the Israelites had to look at an image of the very thing that was causing their suffering: a serpent. It was made of bronze and lifted on a pole. Gazing on this image cured the Israelites of the real serpents' poison.

This bronze serpent prefigures, or looks ahead to, Christ (St. Gregory of Nazianzus). Christ came "in the likeness of sinful flesh" (Rom. 8:3). He *was* like us, in all things but sin (see Heb. 4:15).

Like the Israelites, we need a cure. We need a cure from sin, not to heal our bodies but to heal our souls. And Our Lord was raised up for us on a "pole," the Cross, that all people might look on Him and live.

Those who looked on the serpent were saved in this world. They went on living on earth. But those who look with faith at Our Lord on the Cross, uniting themselves with Him, will live forever in Heaven (St. Ephrem the Syrian). Through His sacrifice, they are healed in their very souls from the effects of their sin.

Prayer

> *Have mercy on me, O Jesus, and help me never to fall into my former sins. From this moment, I will strive sincerely never to sin again. Strengthen me with Your grace, O Lord, that I may faithfully carry out my promise* (St. Francis of Assisi).

Gloria Patri, et Filio, et Spiritui Sancto, sicut erat in principio, et nunc, et semper, et in saecula saeculorum. Amen.	*Glory be to the Father, and to the Son, and to the Holy Spirit, as it was in the beginning, is now, and ever shall be, world without end. Amen.*

For further reflection

* A daily examination of conscience is a time-tested method of strengthening our resolve to avoid sin. How can you remember to examine your conscience every evening, so that you can resolve to avoid falling into the same sins day after day?

* The serpent on the pole looked like, but was not, the poisonous serpent. Christ on the Cross looks like, but is not, sin. Meditate on a crucifix with this in mind.

THURSDAY IN THE THIRD WEEK OF LENT
Christ redeems us from sin

Seventh Station: Jesus Falls the Second Time

Antiphon

℣. *Adoramus Te, Christe,* et benedicimus Tibi, ℟. *Quia per sanctam Crucem Tuam redemisti mundum.*	℣. *We adore You, O Christ, and we praise You,* ℟. *Because by Your holy Cross You have redeemed the world.*

The pain of His wounds and the loss of blood increasing at every step of His way, again His limbs fail him, and He falls to the ground (St. John Henry Newman).

1 John 2:1–6

My little children, I am writing this to you so that you may not sin; but if any one does sin, we have an advocate with the Father, Jesus Christ the righteous; and he is the expiation for our sins, and not for ours only but also for the sins of the whole world. And by this we may be sure that we know him, if we keep his commandments. He who says "I know him" but disobeys his commandments is a liar, and the truth is not in him; but whoever keeps his word, in him truly love for God is perfected. By this we may be sure that we are in him: he who says he abides in him ought to walk in the same way in which he walked.

Meditation

The word *know* is probably one of the most common action words. It's one of the first words students learn in a foreign language because it's so useful. Do you know Dominic? Do you know we're having a picnic? Do you know French?

Do you know Jesus?

A lot of people certainly know *about* Jesus. Anyone can know about Him because we have a historical account of His life. But there is more to the word *know*, especially in the Bible. To know someone, as John here talks about being "sure that we know him," is to "have personal experience of" him (Didymus the Blind). Knowing about Jesus is not enough; we must have experience of Him, as we have experience of our parents and siblings and friends and teachers.

This experience of Our Lord comes from the sacraments and from prayer. In the Mass—which is both—we meet Jesus. He walks among us again, under the appearances of bread and wine and in the Scriptures as they are proclaimed and prayed. We come to know Jesus more every time we pray.

St. John says that if we know Jesus in this way, there will be easy-to-see evidence in our lives. We will keep His commands. It is not enough, John tells us, to hear His word. We must keep it. And as we do so, we will love Him more and more.

Sometimes we fall. Even though we know Him, we fail to keep His commands. Look to Jesus in this second fall on the Way of the Cross. What did He do next? He got up. He lives now in Heaven as our advocate—the one who asks for mercy for us. So ask Him for mercy and grace when you fall. Get up again and keep going on the way.

Prayer

> *Have mercy on me, O Jesus, and help me never to fall into my former sins. From this moment, I will strive sincerely never to sin again. Strengthen me with Your grace, O Lord, that I may faithfully carry out my promise* (St. Francis of Assisi).

Gloria Patri, et Filio, et Spiritui Sancto, sicut erat in principio, et nunc, et semper, et in saecula saeculorum. Amen.	*Glory be to the Father, and to the Son, and to the Holy Spirit, as it was in the beginning, is now, and ever shall be, world without end. Amen.*

For further reflection

- Think about a time when you sinned but immediately repented—by apologizing sincerely or making up for what you did wrong. Thank God for that grace.

- Name people you know who give evidence through the way they live that they truly know Our Lord.

FRIDAY IN THE THIRD WEEK OF LENT

Slaves to sin or servants of God

Seventh Station: Jesus Falls the Second Time

Antiphon

℣. *Adoramus Te, Christe,*
et benedicimus Tibi,
℟. *Quia per sanctam Crucem*
Tuam redemisti mundum.

℣. *We adore You, O Christ,*
and we praise You,
℟. *Because by Your holy Cross*
You have redeemed the world.

The second fall of Jesus under His Cross renews the pain in all the wounds of the head and members of our afflicted Lord (St. Alphonsus Liguori).

Romans 6:16–18
Do you not know that if you yield yourselves to any one as obedient slaves, you are slaves of the one whom you obey, either of sin, which leads to death, or of obedience, which leads to righteousness? But thanks be to God, that you who were once slaves of sin have become obedient from the heart to the standard of teaching to which you were committed, and, having been set free from sin, have become slaves of righteousness.

Meditation
Some people think that ignoring God's commandments is a way to be free. If you have no rules, then you're free, right?

No. St. Paul reminds us here that all men serve some kind of master. And when it comes down to it, we can choose between only two: sin or God. Christ was teaching about this when He said that "no servant can serve two masters" (Luke 16:13). You either strive for obedience to God or you decide that obedience to God doesn't matter.

Ignoring God's commandments doesn't make you free; it makes you a slave to sin. And sin is a terrible master. St. Paul says that when sin is our master, the "paycheck" we receive is death; this is because sin diminishes or takes away altogether the life of God in our souls.

Sin is also the kind of master that is unwilling to let its servants go. The more we serve sin, the harder it is to get away. We tend to fall into sin again and again.

Yet we must not think we have no choice or that falling back into sin is something that can't be helped. St. Paul says that we do have a choice. Will we fail sometimes? Probably. Yet our actions and the choices we make will prove which master we've chosen: sin or God.

What do we do when we sin? Do we rise again, like our Lord on the Way of the Cross? Baptism and Confession clean away the dirt of our falls; Purgatory cleanses sin; but not if we choose sin as our master.

Don't stay in the dirt.

Prayer

> *Have mercy on me, O Jesus, and help me never to fall into my former sins. From this moment, I will strive sincerely never to sin again. Strengthen me with Your grace, O Lord, that I may faithfully carry out my promise* (St. Francis of Assisi).

Gloria Patri, et Filio, et Spiritui Sancto, sicut erat in principio, et nunc, et semper, et in saecula saeculorum. Amen.	*Glory be to the Father, and to the Son, and to the Holy Spirit, as it was in the beginning, is now, and ever shall be, world without end. Amen.*

For further reflection

* Explain this saying of St. Josemaría Escrivá: "Conversion is the matter of a moment. Sanctification is the work of a lifetime."

* Find out what a general confession is and how it is helpful for spiritual growth.

SATURDAY IN THE THIRD WEEK OF LENT

Our forgiveness must be unlimited, like God's

Seventh Station: Jesus Falls the Second Time

Antiphon

℣. *Adoramus Te, Christe,*
et benedicimus Tibi,
℟. *Quia per sanctam Crucem*
Tuam redemisti mundum.

℣. *We adore You, O Christ,*
and we praise You,
℟. *Because by Your holy Cross*
You have redeemed the world.

Overwhelmed by the weight of the Cross, Jesus falls again to the ground.
But the cruel soldiers do not permit Him to rest a moment (St. Francis
of Assisi).

Matthew 18:21–22

Then Peter came up and said to him, "Lord, how often shall my brother
sin against me, and I forgive him? As many as seven times?" Jesus said to
him, "I do not say to you seven times, but seventy times seven."

Meditation

Our Lord's second fall on the Way of the Cross reminds us of how easily
we fall into sin. Every sin offends God, but sin usually also hurts other
people. We ourselves are hurt by the sins of others because the people
around us fall sometimes too.

That's what St. Peter is thinking about when he asks Our Lord about
forgiveness. He has spent enough time with Jesus by now to know that
forgiveness is important. Our Lord has preached about it, and He has
taught His followers to pray using the words "forgive us our trespasses as
we forgive those who trespass against us."

If your brother pushes you, you forgive him. If he does it again, it might
be a little harder to forgive him the second time. So Peter chooses a rather

large number: Shall we forgive seven times, Lord? Seven times seems like a lot. (Maybe he remembers getting pushed around by St. Andrew when they were little.)

Our Lord's answer is as much as to say, "You're not even in the ballpark. If seven times seems like a lot, I'm going to multiply that by something big. Seventy times seven." When was the last time you had to forgive your brother 490 times?

Of course, Jesus doesn't mean 490 times. He doesn't mean that the 491st time your brother pushes you, you no longer have to forgive. He has chosen an essentially countless number (who could keep track?) in order to tell us that forgiveness, to be real, must be unlimited.

As always, Jesus is our model. How many times have you needed His forgiveness? Have you kept count?

Prayer

> *Have mercy on me, O Jesus, and help me never to fall into my former sins. From this moment, I will strive sincerely never to sin again. Strengthen me with Your grace, O Lord, that I may faithfully carry out my promise* (St. Francis of Assisi).

Gloria Patri, et Filio, et Spiritui Sancto, sicut erat in principio, et nunc, et semper, et in saecula saeculorum. Amen.	Glory be to the Father, and to the Son, and to the Holy Spirit, as it was in the beginning, is now, and ever shall be, world without end. Amen.

For further reflection

* God's forgiveness frees us from our sins. There is freedom in the forgiveness we extend to others also. Both the one who sinned and the one who forgives are freed. Why?

* St. Francis says that after Christ falls, "the cruel soldiers do not permit him to rest a moment." How can you liken the soldiers' actions to the response of the evil one when we fall into sin?

VIII

Jesus Meets the Women of Jerusalem

Sorrow

FOURTH SUNDAY OF LENT

"Do not weep for me"

Eighth Station: Jesus Meets the Women of Jerusalem

Antiphon

℣. *Adoramus Te, Christe,*
et benedicimus Tibi,
℟. *Quia per sanctam Crucem*
Tuam redemisti mundum.

℣. *We adore You, O Christ,*
and we praise You,
℟. *Because by Your holy Cross*
You have redeemed the world.

At the sight of the sufferings of Jesus, the Holy Women are so pierced with grief that they cry out and bewail Him, careless what happens to them by so doing (St. John Henry Newman).

Luke 23:27–31

And there followed him a great multitude of the people, and of women who bewailed and lamented him. But Jesus turning to them said, "Daughters of Jerusalem, do not weep for me, but weep for yourselves and for your children. For behold, the days are coming when they will say, 'Blessed are the barren, and the wombs that never bore, and the breasts that never gave suck!' Then they will begin to say to the mountains, 'Fall on us'; and to the hills, 'Cover us.' For if they do this when the wood is green, what will happen when it is dry?"

Meditation

Imagine yourself in Jerusalem all those centuries ago, following Our Lord from a distance along the Way of the Cross. Would your heart not break?

It was natural for the women of Jerusalem to weep when they saw the immense suffering of so good and innocent a man. But Christ tells them: don't cry. This may seem strange, but He explains Himself.

First, as He taught many times, joy would come after His suffering, a joy that could never be compared with the sorrow of this day, this Friday that we call "Good" because of what it accomplished for us. Christ's death is not a reason to mourn because it is the very source of all joy (St. Athanasius).

Second, Jesus prophesies about times to come (St. Cyril of Alexandria). He says that there will be hard times when He is gone. Things will get so difficult that people will think it would be better for an earthquake to happen than to suffer what they are suffering. He says that what the soldiers are doing to Him, in spite of all the miracles He did during His life, shows that His followers, too, will endure great suffering (St. Ephrem the Syrian).

It is only natural that we, "the dry wood," should sometimes suffer. The very word *Christian*, which we call ourselves, means that we want to be "little Christs" in this world. That means we want to be a version of someone who was "despised and rejected by men" (Isa. 53:3) and ultimately killed. Be not sorrowful in suffering, but take joy in what you know follows it. "Joy comes with the morning" (Ps. 30:5).

Prayer

> *My Jesus, laden with sorrows, I weep for the sins I have committed against You — because of the punishment I deserve for them and, still more, because of the displeasure they have caused You, who have loved me with an infinite love. Have mercy on me* (St. Alphonsus Liguori).

Gloria Patri, et Filio, et Spiritui Sancto, sicut erat in principio, et nunc, et semper, et in saecula saeculorum. Amen.	*Glory be to the Father, and to the Son, and to the Holy Spirit, as it was in the beginning, is now, and ever shall be, world without end. Amen.*

For further reflection

* Read and ponder St. Francis's description of what perfect joy is.[2]

* Try it: the next time someone offends you, say "thank you" in your heart as you call to mind your own sinfulness, Christ's suffering for you, and God's infinite mercy.

MONDAY IN THE FOURTH WEEK OF LENT
Christ cautions about coming persecutions

Eighth Station: Jesus Meets the Women of Jerusalem

Antiphon

℣. *Adoramus Te, Christe,*
et benedicimus Tibi,
℟. *Quia per sanctam Crucem*
Tuam redemisti mundum.

℣. *We adore You, O Christ,*
and we praise You,
℟. *Because by Your holy Cross*
You have redeemed the world.

The women weep with compassion seeing Jesus so distressed and dripping with blood as He walks along (St. Alphonsus Liguori).

Matthew 10:24–25

[Jesus said:] "A disciple is not above his teacher, nor a servant above his master; it is enough for the disciple to be like his teacher, and the servant like his master. If they have called the master of the house Beelzebul, how much more will they malign those of his household."

Meditation

When Christ spoke to the women of Jerusalem about the hard times to come, it wasn't the first time He predicted difficulties for His followers. Our Lord prepared His followers for hardship many times.

It helps to know what's coming. Have you ever had to have stitches for a deep cut? The doctor probably let you know what was going to happen at every step: "I'm going to clean the cut now"; "I'm going to give you a shot to numb your arm so you don't feel the stitches." If we know what's going to happen, we can prepare ourselves to endure it.

What if, before you got those stitches, you had watched your dad get stitches? Maybe he cut himself deeply and you went along to the doctor. You watched while your dad bravely endured the cleaning, the shot, the stitches. He probably looked at you once in a while with a smile to let you know he was doing okay.

These things are what Christ provided for us with regard to the persecution we will face as His followers (St. Hilary). First, He told us what was going to happen. Second, in His life, suffering, and death, He gave us a model of how to endure it.

You don't need to be sad when you are rejected for Christ's sake. Look up at Him, your model and your Lord, with a smile, and know that your Teacher is pleased with your faithfulness.

Prayer

> *My Jesus, laden with sorrows, I weep for the sins I have committed against You — because of the punishment I deserve for them and, still more, because of the displeasure they have caused You, who have loved me with an infinite love. Have mercy on me (St. Alphonsus Liguori).*

Gloria Patri, et Filio, et Spiritui Sancto, sicut erat in principio, et nunc, et semper, et in saecula saeculorum. Amen.	*Glory be to the Father, and to the Son, and to the Holy Spirit, as it was in the beginning, is now, and ever shall be, world without end. Amen.*

For further reflection

* Describe someone you know who seems to model himself or herself after Our Lord. What characteristics and deeds of this person are most Christlike?

* Consider this saying of St. Josemaría Escrivá: "How I wish your bearing and conversation were such that, on seeing or hearing you, people would say: This man reads the life of Jesus Christ."

TUESDAY IN THE FOURTH WEEK OF LENT

Sorrow for sin means committing to avoiding sin

Eighth Station: Jesus Meets the Women of Jerusalem

Antiphon

℣. *Adoramus Te, Christe,*
et benedicimus Tibi,
℟. *Quia per sanctam Crucem*
Tuam redemisti mundum.

℣. *We adore You, O Christ,*
and we praise You,
℟. *Because by Your holy Cross*
You have redeemed the world.

Moved by compassion, these devoted women weep over our suffering Savior. But He turns to them and says, "Weep not for me, but weep for yourselves and your children" (St. Francis of Assisi).

2 Corinthians 7:9–10

As it is, I rejoice, not because you were grieved, but because you were grieved into repenting; for you felt a godly grief, so that you suffered no loss through us. For godly grief produces a repentance that leads to salvation and brings no regret, but worldly grief produces death.

Meditation

When Our Lord instructed the women of Jerusalem not to weep for Him, did He mean that there is no cause at all to be sorrowful in this life? No. In today's passage, St. Paul tells us about the one kind of sorrow that is useful: sorrow for our sins (St. Augustine).

This kind of sorrow, the kind that is good and valuable, is a step toward God; other kinds of sorrow are often steps away from him (St. Ambrose). This is a hard truth to live out. When we suffer—say we strike out every time we're up to bat, or we burn the cookies, or our cat runs away from home—something has not gone the way we wanted. It is natural to be disappointed and sad, and those feelings aren't wrong. But we offer those feelings up to God and acknowledge that He reigns. He's using all events in our lives as steps toward Him, even when we can't see how.

Sorrow for sin is different from sorrow about not getting our way. Sorrow for sin gives us a deep desire to make a promise to God. We promise that we will do everything we can to keep from sinning again. We make this promise in the Act of Contrition: I will "sin no more and avoid the near occasion of sin."

Sorrow about not getting our way is different in another way too. Often, it lingers on and on. Even when it's short-lived, it serves no real purpose.

Sorrow for sin, on the other hand, both has a purpose and comes to an end. It comes to an end because it is only one step on the path to holiness. It makes us resolve to avoid sin in the future and helps us reconcile ourselves with God, especially through the sacrament of Confession. We move on from this sorrow to repentance and then to joy (St. John Chrysostom).

Prayer

> *My Jesus, laden with sorrows, I weep for the sins I have committed against You—because of the punishment I deserve for them and, still more, because of the displeasure they have caused You, who have loved me with an infinite love. Have mercy on me* (St. Alphonsus Liguori).

Gloria Patri, et Filio, et Spiritui Sancto, sicut erat in principio, et nunc, et semper, et in saecula saeculorum. Amen.	*Glory be to the Father, and to the Son, and to the Holy Spirit, as it was in the beginning, is now, and ever shall be, world without end. Amen.*

For further reflection

* Besides examining your conscience and confessing your sins to a priest, what three other things are needed for a good confession (*Baltimore Catechism*)?

* Pope Benedict XVI said that humility was a key step in the conversion of St. Mary Magdalene. Why is humility so important for repentance?

IX

Jesus Falls
the Third Time

Repentance

WEDNESDAY IN THE FOURTH WEEK OF LENT
Cain compounds sin with sin

Ninth Station: Jesus Falls the Third Time

Antiphon

℣. *Adoramus Te, Christe,*
et benedicimus Tibi,
℟. *Quia per sanctam Crucem*
Tuam redemisti mundum.

℣. *We adore You, O Christ,*
and we praise You,
℟. *Because by Your holy Cross*
You have redeemed the world.

Our Lord falls for the third time, on the slope leading up to Calvary,
with only forty or fifty paces between Him and the summit. Jesus can no
longer stay on His feet: His strength has failed Him, and He lies on the
ground in utter exhaustion (St. Josemaría Escrivá).

Genesis 4:3–7
In the course of time Cain brought to the LORD an offering of the fruit of the
ground, and Abel brought of the firstlings of his flock and of their fat por-
tions. And the LORD had regard for Abel and his offering, but for Cain and
his offering he had no regard. So Cain was very angry, and his countenance
fell. The LORD said to Cain, "Why are you angry, and why has your countenance fallen? If you do well, will you not be accepted? And if you do not do
well, sin is couching at the door; its desire is for you, but you must master it."

Meditation
The third fall of Our Lord on the Way of the Cross is a painful reminder
that we tend toward sin again and again.

We think of Cain as the man who killed his own brother. But we must
look back before that event to see how it happened. Cain's sin did not begin
with murdering Abel; he had already committed lesser sins (Origen). He
had been careless in choosing an offering for God. Then, when he was

corrected by God—gently!—He could have chosen to do better next time. But he chose to become bitter.

When God chided Cain for his poor offering, it was an opportunity. Cain had the chance to change his ways, but he did not choose that path. When our sins come to light—in our conscience or when they are pointed out to us—this is an opportunity. Will we choose the path of repentance for our sin, or will we resist God's correction?

The evil one is attentive to see how we will choose, as he was attentive to Cain (St. Ephrem the Syrian). Your guardian angel is prompting you to resolve to do right rather than to become bitter about your error and its consequences.

Christ shows us what to do. He got up. He went on.

Will you fall again? Perhaps. But God will use even this to lead you on toward salvation, if you listen to Him and allow Him to work in you (Fr. Jacques Philippe).

Prayer

O Jesus, may I hate sin and unite myself to You, taking the holy Cross into my arms, so that I, in my turn, may fulfill Your will (St. Josemaría Escrivá). *Never permit me to offend You again. Grant that I may love You always, and then do with me as You will* (St. Alphonsus Liguori).

Gloria Patri, et Filio, et Spiritui Sancto, sicut erat in principio, et nunc, et semper, et in saecula saeculorum. Amen.	Glory be to the Father, and to the Son, and to the Holy Spirit, as it was in the beginning, is now, and ever shall be, world without end. Amen.

For further reflection

* Can you think of another incident in the Bible when bitterness about one's wrongdoing led someone on to greater sin?

* How can Confession help "stop the cycle" of sin, bitterness, and greater sin?

THURSDAY IN THE FOURTH WEEK OF LENT
Judas despairs

Ninth Station: Jesus Falls the Third Time

Antiphon

℣. *Adoramus Te, Christe,*	℣. *We adore You, O Christ,*
et benedicimus Tibi,	*and we praise You,*
℟. *Quia per sanctam Crucem*	℟. *Because by Your holy Cross*
Tuam redemisti mundum.	*You have redeemed the world.*

*Exhausted at the foot of Calvary, Jesus falls for the third time. How pain-
fully must have been reopened all the wounds of his tender body by these
repeated falls* (St. Francis of Assisi).

Matthew 27:3–5

When Judas, his betrayer, saw that he was condemned, he repented and
brought back the thirty pieces of silver to the chief priests and the elders,
saying, "I have sinned in betraying innocent blood." They said, "What is
that to us? See to it yourself." And throwing down the pieces of silver in
the temple, he departed; and he went and hanged himself.

Meditation

As we consider the third fall of Jesus on the Way of the Cross, we are thinking about what happens when we sin. What should happen? We know that
we should feel sorry. But today we learn from Judas that feeling terribly sorry
about what we've done is not enough on its own (St. John Chrysostom).
Feeling how awful it is that we've sinned is a dangerous place to get stuck.
We must always recognize this feeling as a stepping stone toward something
else: asking forgiveness.

Judas knew how serious his sin was. He realized it within hours of
betraying Jesus. Cain had to be told he had done wrong when he made a

poor offering. Judas seems to have realized his sin for himself. Like Cain, Judas still had a choice once he knew he had sinned. His sorrow could have led him to reconciliation. Instead, he chose despair: believing that his sin was too great to be forgiven; believing that there was no hope for him.

At first, Judas seemed to try to make up for what he did by giving the silver back. But we cannot "pay back" our sin in that way—not without asking forgiveness of God and the person we have hurt (St. Jerome). It wasn't the temple leaders whom Judas needed to tell he was wrong. It was Jesus.

Imagine if Judas had gone to Our Lord, perhaps while he was on the Way of the Cross. Imagine him throwing himself in the dirt to beg for Christ's forgiveness. What do you think would have happened next?

Prayer

> O Jesus, may I hate sin and unite myself to You, taking the holy Cross into my arms, so that I, in my turn, may fulfill Your will (St. Josemaría Escrivá). Never permit me to offend You again. Grant that I may love You always, and then do with me as You will (St. Alphonsus Liguori).

Gloria Patri, et Filio, et Spiritui Sancto, sicut erat in principio, et nunc, et semper, et in saecula saeculorum. Amen.	*Glory be to the Father, and to the Son, and to the Holy Spirit, as it was in the beginning, is now, and ever shall be, world without end. Amen.*

For further reflection

* If we were to steal something, we would do penance by giving the item back or paying for it, as well as apologizing to the owner. How can we do penance for a sin such as being inattentive at Mass or being disrespectful to our parents?

* There are many versions of the Act of Contrition. Find several to compare. What elements do they have in common?

FRIDAY IN THE FOURTH WEEK OF LENT

Peter mourns his betrayal of Christ

Ninth Station: Jesus Falls the Third Time

Antiphon

℣. *Adoramus Te, Christe,* *et benedicimus Tibi,* ℞. *Quia per sanctam Crucem* *Tuam redemisti mundum.*	℣. *We adore You, O Christ,* *and we praise You,* ℞. *Because by Your holy Cross* *You have redeemed the world.*

Jesus has now almost reached the top of Calvary; but before He gains the very spot where He is to be crucified, again He falls, and He is again dragged up and goaded onward by the brutal soldiers (St. John Henry Newman).

Luke 22:54–62

Then they seized him and led him away, bringing him into the high priest's house. Peter followed at a distance; and when they had kindled a fire in the middle of the courtyard and sat down together, Peter sat among them. Then a maid, seeing him as he sat in the light and gazing at him, said, "This man also was with him." But he denied it, saying, "Woman, I do not know him." And a little later someone else saw him and said, "You also are one of them." But Peter said, "Man, I am not." And after an interval of about an hour still another insisted, saying, "Certainly this man also was with him; for he is a Galilean." But Peter said, "Man, I do not know what you are saying." And immediately, while he was still speaking, the cock crowed. And the Lord turned and looked at Peter. And Peter remembered the word of the Lord, how he had said to him, "Before the cock crows today, you will deny me three times." And he went out and wept bitterly.

Meditation

St. Peter is the apostle we get to know best as we read the Gospels. He's outgoing, impetuous, a natural leader. He speaks his mind, sometimes without thinking too hard about the words he's saying. Many of us know someone like Peter. Some of us *are* someone like Peter!

In a grand gesture, Peter promises the Lord at the Last Supper that he will stay with Him always. He will never fail Him, even if everyone else does. Does this seem bold and unlikely? Not for Peter! He had always been able to do what he set out to do. How could following Jesus to the end be any different? He had been brave already; he had endured suffering and rejection; he had worked hard these three years. He could do it!

He could not do it. Naturally, he became afraid after the Lord was arrested. He knew quite well the position of a poor Jewish ex-fisherman in relation to the powerful people surrounding him: Roman officials, the Jewish governor, the Pharisees, the temple guards. He was nothing compared with them.

Being afraid, how natural it was for him to lie to the young woman who said he was a friend of Jesus. Yes, it is "natural" to us to sin—in terms of the nature we inherited from Adam and Eve.

Then Peter repents. When? We find that it happens when "Christ looked at him." For once, Peter says nothing, for words would only have made things worse (St. Ambrose). He simply weeps.

Jesus fell three times under the weight of the Cross, but those falls are not where the story ends. There is always more. We'll see more of Peter's story, too, after this fall.

Prayer

> *O Jesus, may I hate sin and unite myself to You, taking the holy Cross into my arms, so that I, in my turn, may fulfill Your will* (St. Josemaría Escrivá). *Never permit me to offend You again. Grant that I may love You always, and then do with me as You will* (St. Alphonsus Liguori).

Gloria Patri, et Filio, et Spiritui Sancto, sicut erat in principio, et nunc, et semper, et in saecula saeculorum. Amen.	*Glory be to the Father, and to the Son, and to the Holy Spirit, as it was in the beginning, is now, and ever shall be, world without end. Amen.*

For further reflection

* Sometimes, it is when "Christ looks at us" that we finally understand how we've sinned. What can we do that invites Him to look at us?

* Why does one lie often lead to others?

SATURDAY IN THE FOURTH WEEK OF LENT
Christ forgives Peter

Ninth Station: Jesus Falls the Third Time

Antiphon

℣. *Adoramus Te, Christe,*
et benedicimus Tibi,
℟. *Quia per sanctam Crucem*
Tuam redemisti mundum.

℣. *We adore You, O Christ,*
and we praise You,
℟. *Because by Your holy Cross*
You have redeemed the world.

Jesus falls for the third time. He is extremely weak, and the cruelty of His executioners is excessive; they try to hasten His steps though He hardly has strength to move (St. Alphonsus Liguori).

John 21:15–19

When they had finished breakfast, Jesus said to Simon Peter, "Simon, son of John, do you love me more than these?" He said to him, "Yes, Lord; you know that I love you." He said to him, "Feed my lambs." A second time he said to him, "Simon, son of John, do you love me?" He said to him, "Yes, Lord; you know that I love you." He said to him, "Tend my sheep." He said to him the third time, "Simon, son of John, do you love me?" Peter was grieved because he said to him the third time, "Do you love me?" And he said to him, "Lord, you know everything; you know that I love you." Jesus said to him, "Feed my sheep. Truly, truly, I say to you, when you were young, you girded yourself and walked where you would; but when you are old, you will stretch out your hands, and another will gird you and carry you where you do not wish to go." (This he said to show by what death he was to glorify God.) And after this he said to him, "Follow me."

Meditation

We see Christ fall, and we see Him rise again. We know that when we fall into sin, we must rise again. This happens through the sacrament of Confession, in which our sincere sorrow for our sins is like a key that unlocks a treasure chest. That chest is filled with the graces Christ won on the Cross, and in the sacraments, these treasures are given to us, God's children and heirs. In the sacrament of Confession, Christ, through the priest, gives us the gift of forgiveness of our sins.

After His Resurrection, we see Our Lord give this gift to St. Peter in a very moving way. What a joy for Peter to have this burden lifted from his heart! But did the removal of it hurt a little bit? Yes, it did (St. John Chrysostom). Christ asked Peter not just once but three times "Do you love me?" If your mom or dad asked you this question once, you'd happily answer yes. By the third time, you'd wonder what you had done wrong.

Peter knew well what he had done wrong, and it hurt to remember it. But Christ did this to erase that betrayal. Not only that, but Christ hearkened back to those bold promises Peter made before he could fulfill them: the promises to stay with Christ always and never to leave Him. When he first said those things, Peter did not have the grace of Christ's death to make them truly possible. Now he had that grace. And Christ let him know: *I understand that you wish to die for me. I know you meant it when you said it, but you were not able to do it then. Now you are able, because of what I have done, and furthermore, I promise that you* will *die for me* (St. John Chrysostom).

Prayer

> *O Jesus, may I hate sin and unite myself to You, taking the holy Cross into my arms, so that I, in my turn, may fulfill Your will* (St. Josemaría Escrivá). *Never permit me to offend You again. Grant that I may love You always, and then do with me as You will* (St. Alphonsus Liguori).

Gloria Patri, et Filio, et Spiritui Sancto, sicut erat in principio, et nunc, et semper, et in saecula saeculorum. Amen.	*Glory be to the Father, and to the Son, and to the Holy Spirit, as it was in the beginning, is now, and ever shall be, world without end. Amen.*

For further reflection

* Sometimes we are given the grace of feeling lightness of heart following a good confession. Have you ever experienced this?

* Why is it that martyrdom, rather than a terrible fate to be avoided, is seen by St. Peter (and countless others) as the greatest honor this life can offer?

X

Jesus Is Stripped
of His Garments

Poverty

FIFTH SUNDAY OF LENT
Jesus has nothing left but the Cross

Tenth Station: Jesus Is Stripped of His Garments

Antiphon

℣. *Adoramus Te, Christe,*
et benedicimus Tibi,
℟. *Quia per sanctam Crucem*
Tuam redemisti mundum.

℣. *We adore You, O Christ,*
and we praise You,
℟. *Because by Your holy Cross*
You have redeemed the world.

Arriving at Calvary, Jesus is cruelly deprived of His garments. How painful the stripping must be because the clothing adheres to His wounded body, such that removing it tears parts of His flesh away. Jesus dies possessed of nothing (St. Francis of Assisi).

Matthew 27:33–36

And when they came to a place called Golgotha (which means the place of a skull), they offered him wine to drink, mingled with gall; but when he tasted it, he would not drink it. And when they had crucified him, they divided his garments among them by casting lots; then they sat down and kept watch over him there.

Meditation

The life of Jesus is at an end. And what possessions does He have to leave behind Him? Does He have a house, or money, or maybe a fine horse? No. Not even His clothes are left to Him. All that He has is the Cross (St. Josemaría Escrivá).

Jesus shows us in this station that, to be like Him, we must be stripped of the things of this world. We see how little these things mean: we don't even care about them when we gaze at Jesus on the Cross.

Brothers and sisters in the religious life live this out. They know that attachment to *things* limits our attachment to Christ. Those in the religious life take a vow of poverty and imitate Jesus in this station very completely. Their clothes—their habits—are not even their own.

The trouble for most of us is that when we stop gazing at Jesus on the Cross, those things of earth—games and clothes, movies and money, even being well-liked by others—those things seem so important! And it's tricky because we need some things of the earth to live on earth!

We must understand the temptation of giving those things importance they do not deserve because they deserve very little. (Look at Jesus on the Cross!) The things that we seek on earth for their own sake are like ropes that tie us to the ground—whether you're seven years old and begging for the last cookie or you're thirty-seven and have your heart set on a bigger, better house. They're ropes that tie us down here, when Jesus is *up there*—on the Cross, totally poor! How will we climb to Him if we are tied down with so many ropes?

Prayer

> *O Jesus, by the torment You suffered in being stripped of Your garments, help me to strip myself of all attachment to the things of the earth, that I may place all my love in You, who are so worthy of my love* (St. Alphonsus Liguori).

Gloria Patri, et Filio, et Spiritui Sancto, sicut erat in principio, et nunc, et semper, et in saecula saeculorum. Amen.	*Glory be to the Father, and to the Son, and to the Holy Spirit, as it was in the beginning, is now, and ever shall be, world without end. Amen.*

For further reflection

* What are some practices that can help you become more spiritually poor during Lent?

* How does this station remind us of the humility of Our Lord in the exposition of the Most Blessed Sacrament?

MONDAY IN THE FIFTH WEEK OF LENT
Store up treasure in Heaven

Tenth Station: Jesus Is Stripped of His Garments

Antiphon

℣. *Adoramus Te, Christe,*
et benedicimus Tibi,
℟. *Quia per sanctam Crucem*
Tuam redemisti mundum.

℣. *We adore You, O Christ,*
and we praise You,
℟. *Because by Your holy Cross*
You have redeemed the world.

Jesus is violently stripped of His clothes by the soldiers. The inner garments adhere to His torn flesh, and the soldiers tear them off so roughly that the skin comes with them (St. Alphonsus Liguori).

Matthew 6:19–21

[Jesus said:] "Do not lay up for yourselves treasures on earth, where moth and rust consume and where thieves break in and steal, but lay up for yourselves treasures in heaven, where neither moth nor rust consumes and where thieves do not break in and steal. For where your treasure is, there will your heart be also."

Meditation

How easy it is for us to become distracted by things. Sometimes the things of the earth serve a good purpose. We need food and clothing. The student needs books to carry out his vocation as a student; the gardener and the carpenter need tools; the cook needs pots and pans.

We are contemplating Christ's final hours—and now He is stripped of everything He had on this earth. Can you imagine in your final moments looking back on your life to see that it was spent chasing after things: toys or cars or furniture? How sad if, when we are stripped of all we have, as every person is at the moment of death, that stripping reveals barns full of *stuff* that will simply pass away in time (see Luke 12:20). All that energy for what the moth will one day destroy.

There is a difference between owning things and treasuring them. Christ says that what we treasure calls to our hearts. He asks us to put all our effort into building up our treasure chests in Heaven. That treasure will never go away.

The Church tells us exactly how we can store up the right kind of treasure. First, consider all your goods—whether toys and books or hobbies and friendships—as owned by God. Ask Him to do with them as He pleases (Thomas à Kempis). Second, pray; do good works; frequent the sacraments; gain indulgences. Each of these things can give us another jewel in our heavenly treasure box.

Prayer

> *O Jesus, by the torment You suffered in being stripped of Your garments, help me to strip myself of all attachment to the things of the earth, that I may place all my love in You, who are so worthy of my love* (St. Alphonsus Liguori).

Gloria Patri, et Filio, et Spiritui Sancto, sicut erat in principio, et nunc, et semper, et in saecula saeculorum. Amen.	*Glory be to the Father, and to the Son, and to the Holy Spirit, as it was in the beginning, is now, and ever shall be, world without end. Amen.*

For further reflection

⁕ The pain Our Lord experienced in the stripping of His garments was excruciating. Have you ever felt hurt when you had to let go of some good of this life?

⁕ Consider what you are attached to. What gets in the way of giving your entire heart to God?

TUESDAY IN THE FIFTH WEEK OF LENT
He must increase, and I must decrease

Tenth Station: Jesus Is Stripped of His Garments

Antiphon

℣. *Adoramus Te, Christe,*	℣. *We adore You, O Christ,*
et benedicimus Tibi,	*and we praise You,*
℟. *Quia per sanctam Crucem*	℟. *Because by Your holy Cross*
Tuam redemisti mundum.	*You have redeemed the world.*

At length, He has arrived at the place of sacrifice, and they begin to prepare Him for the Cross. His garments are torn from His bleeding body, and He, the Holy of Holiest, stands exposed to the gaze of the coarse and scoffing crowd (St. John Henry Newman).

John 3:26–30

And they came to John, and said to him, "Rabbi, he who was with you beyond the Jordan, to whom you bore witness, here he is, baptizing, and all are going to him." John answered, "No one can receive anything except what is given him from heaven. You yourselves bear me witness, that I said, I am not the Christ, but I have been sent before him. He who has the bride is the bridegroom; the friend of the bridegroom, who stands and hears him, rejoices greatly at the bridegroom's voice; therefore this joy of mine is now full. He must increase, but I must decrease."

Meditation

John the Baptist had a noble mission, and he set out to complete it with all his strength. He gained many followers. Here we see some of them appealing to him: "This other man, this Jesus—people are following Him instead of you! The One you made famous—He was just one of your followers because you baptized Him—He's getting more attention than you!" (St. John Chrysostom).

They figured John's pride would make him upset about all the notice Jesus was getting (St. Augustine). They thought they could make John jealous because they themselves were jealous (St. John Chrysostom).

But John was not attached to his work in that way. Not even his God-given mission in life was more important to him than God Himself. He had been stripped of such attachments; no such ropes held him down. As we see in this station, our Lord was utterly poor, yet He was totally free. John also was poor and therefore free—not just poor because he didn't own many things, but spiritually poor: he wasn't attached even to his own mission (St. Cyril of Alexandria).

These followers of John wanted his reputation to increase. But John cautioned them that the "increase" we must seek is the increase of Christ.

John knew the day was at hand when such a thing can happen within each follower of God. Christ's death on the Cross would make it possible. Through Baptism—and the grace that flows from Christ's sacrifice—He lives in us. Through the graces of the Eucharist and all the sacraments, Christ can increase: He can live in us more and more (see Gal. 2:20).

Prayer

> *O Jesus, by the torment You suffered in being stripped of Your garments, help me to strip myself of all attachment to the things of the earth, that I may place all my love in You, who are so worthy of my love* (St. Alphonsus Liguori).

Gloria Patri, et Filio, et Spiritui Sancto, sicut erat in principio, et nunc, et semper, et in saecula saeculorum. Amen.	*Glory be to the Father, and to the Son, and to the Holy Spirit, as it was in the beginning, is now, and ever shall be, world without end. Amen.*

For further reflection

* What did Our Lord mean when He said, "Among those born of women there has risen no one greater than John the Baptist; yet he who is least in the kingdom of heaven is greater than he" (Matt. 11:11)?

* What are some ways to fight jealousy when it rises in our hearts? How is jealousy sometimes disguised as something else?

XI

Jesus Is Nailed to the Cross

The Cross

WEDNESDAY IN THE FIFTH WEEK OF LENT
The Crucifixion at Golgotha

Eleventh Station: Jesus Is Nailed to the Cross

Antiphon

℣. *Adoramus Te, Christe,*	℣. *We adore You, O Christ,*
et benedicimus Tibi,	*and we praise You,*
℟. *Quia per sanctam Crucem*	℟. *Because by Your holy Cross*
Tuam redemisti mundum.	*You have redeemed the world.*

The Cross is laid on the ground and Jesus stretched upon it, and then, swaying heavily to and fro, it is, after much exertion, jerked upright into the hole in the ground. There He hangs, a perplexity to the crowd; a terror to evil spirits; the wonder, the awe, even the joy, and the adoration of the holy angels (St. John Henry Newman).

Luke 23:33–34

And when they came to the place which is called The Skull, there they crucified him, and the criminals, one on the right and one on the left. And Jesus said, "Father, forgive them; for they know not what they do." And they cast lots to divide his garments.

Meditation

Long before Jesus was born, Isaiah prophesied about His death, saying Our Lord would be "numbered with the transgressors" (Isa. 53:12). In other words, people would call Him a criminal.

The devil hoped that the true identity and mission of Our Lord would be covered up by the fact that He died like a criminal (St. John Chrysostom). Who could believe someone special would die a humiliating death alongside two thieves? For it was well known that "cursed be every one who hangs on a tree" (Gal. 3:13).

Jesus shows us that the meaning of His death is indeed a mystery to those who killed Him. When He forgives them, He mentions their ignorance: "they know not what they do." Nevertheless, the devil's attempt to hide what was really happening on Golgotha was a failure (St. John Chrysostom). Such a thing was impossible to do.

Even the name of the place points to Christ's mission: The Skull. What is a skull but a head? And who is Jesus but the head of all angelic powers (Col. 2:10); the head of the Body, the Church (Col. 1:18); and the head of every man (1 Cor. 11:3)? The "head" suffered in "the place of the skull" to win our redemption (St. Cyril of Jerusalem).

The Jews believed Golgotha was the place where Adam had long ago been buried. What more fitting place for Our Lord, who had taken on Himself the curse of Adam, to be "hanged on a tree"? The curse of Adam began with a tree. Now, nailed to a tree, Christ is indeed cursed. He has taken our curse on Himself in order to destroy it forever (St. Cyril of Alexandria).

Prayer

> *O Jesus, I give myself to You entirely. Nail my heart to the Cross, that it may always remain there to love You and never leave You again* (St. Alphonsus Liguori).

Gloria Patri, et Filio, et Spiritui Sancto, sicut erat in principio, et nunc, et semper, et in saecula saeculorum. Amen.	*Glory be to the Father, and to the Son, and to the Holy Spirit, as it was in the beginning, is now, and ever shall be, world without end. Amen.*

For further reflection

* Why does St. John Henry Newman say that Christ on the Cross was "a terror to evil spirits"? Why was He the "joy … of the holy angels"?

* Eve picked the fruit that was forbidden from the tree in the Garden of Eden. What does it mean to say that Christ put the fruit back on the tree?

THURSDAY IN THE FIFTH WEEK OF LENT

The two thieves respond to Jesus

Eleventh Station: Jesus Is Nailed to the Cross

Antiphon

℣. *Adoramus Te, Christe,*	℣. *We adore You, O Christ,*
et benedicimus Tibi,	*and we praise You,*
℟. *Quia per sanctam Crucem*	℟. *Because by Your holy Cross*
Tuam redemisti mundum.	*You have redeemed the world.*

Now they are crucifying Our Lord and, with Him, two thieves, one on His right and one on His left. And Jesus says, "Father, forgive them, for they do not know what they are doing" (St. Josemaría Escrivá).

Luke 23:39–43

One of the criminals who were hanged railed at him, saying, "Are you not the Christ? Save yourself and us!" But the other rebuked him, saying, "Do you not fear God, since you are under the same sentence of condemnation? And we indeed justly; for we are receiving the due reward of our deeds; but this man has done nothing wrong." And he said, "Jesus, remember me when you come in your kingly power." And he said to him, "Truly, I say to you, today you will be with me in Paradise."

Meditation

Think about it for a moment: while Our Lord is dying on the Cross, the bad thief scolds him for *not saving him.*

The second thief corrects the first: "This is what we deserve." He looks at Christ and sees not shame and guilt but dignity and innocence (St. Ephrem the Syrian). He sees something noble and kingly in Our Lord, something that Judas, in three years of following Him, had missed—something completely invisible to the bad thief. And Christ responds not as a man hanging on a tree but as a king on his throne of power (St. Leo the Great).

We, too, are these thieves. Sometimes we are blinded by our own sin. We can't see Christ for who He is, and we might even scold Him: Why aren't You helping me? We must change our viewpoint and be like the good thief: seeing our own sin for what it is and seeing Christ for who He is.

The good thief knew he had done wrong, and he knew where he was as a result. When we have done wrong, we have to admit it. We have to feel sorry. And then we have to confess it out loud to Our Lord, asking Him to bring us into His Kingdom.

We do this in Confession: we examine our consciences to recall what we've done wrong; we realize that our sins deserve punishment; we ask Our Lord, through the priest, to bring us to His Kingdom through the forgiveness of our sins.

And we trust that He can and will. Our King reigns from a Cross, and *there* is all our hope for salvation.

Prayer

> O Jesus, I give myself to You entirely. Nail my heart to the Cross, that it may always remain there to love You and never leave You again (St. Alphonsus Liguori).

Gloria Patri, et Filio, et Spiritui Sancto, sicut erat in principio, et nunc, et semper, et in saecula saeculorum. Amen.	Glory be to the Father, and to the Son, and to the Holy Spirit, as it was in the beginning, is now, and ever shall be, world without end. Amen.

For further reflection

* What is the meaning of these words of St. Alphonsus Liguori: "Nail my heart to the Cross"?

* Is it possible that the good thief read the sign hanging above Christ's head? How might doing so have influenced his words to Our Lord?

FRIDAY IN THE FIFTH WEEK OF LENT

The King of the Jews

Eleventh Station: Jesus Is Nailed to the Cross

Antiphon

℣. *Adoramus Te, Christe,*	℣. *We adore You, O Christ,*
et benedicimus Tibi,	*and we praise You,*
℟. *Quia per sanctam Crucem*	℟. *Because by Your holy Cross*
Tuam redemisti mundum.	*You have redeemed the world.*

Jesus is thrown down upon the Cross. He stretches out His arms and offers to His eternal Father the sacrifice of His life for our salvation. They nail His hands and feet, and then, raising the Cross, leave Him to die in anguish (St. Alphonsus Liguori).

John 19:19–22

Pilate also wrote a title and put it on the Cross; it read, "Jesus of Nazareth, the King of the Jews." Many of the Jews read this title, for the place where Jesus was crucified was near the city; and it was written in Hebrew, in Latin, and in Greek. The chief priests of the Jews then said to Pilate, "Do not write, 'The King of the Jews,' but, 'This man said, I am King of the Jews.'" Pilate answered, "What I have written I have written."

Meditation

When our Lord was born, Magi came from the East to honor Him, the newborn King. Now, at the end of His life, a man from the West, Pilate of the Roman Empire, also honors Him with the title King (St. Augustine). Truly, Jesus came for all men (see Luke 24:45–47).

Pilate commands that these words be written over the head of Our Lord on the Cross: "Jesus of Nazareth, King of the Jews." It seems that Pilate finally gets to say what he really thinks about all that has been happening to this man, Jesus. He never wanted Him to be crucified, but he came to feel he had no choice. Yet his heart told him that the man was no criminal.

The sign he orders is like a label for the Cross. What is this thing, Pilate? What has this man done? According to Pilate, His only crime is that He is a King (St. John Chrysostom).

Ordinarily, when a king dies, he ceases to be king. A new king must be crowned because a dead king's power has ended. Not so for Our Lord. His title of King was as true after His death as it was before (St. Augustine). It is true today and always.

As you imagine Our Lord nailed to the Cross and raised up, see your King. This King of ours is ascending His throne, and His kingdom will never end.

Prayer

> *O Jesus, I give myself to You entirely. Nail my heart to the Cross, that it may always remain there to love You and never leave You again* (St. Alphonsus Liguori).

Gloria Patri, et Filio, et Spiritui Sancto, sicut erat in principio, et nunc, et semper, et in saecula saeculorum. Amen.	*Glory be to the Father, and to the Son, and to the Holy Spirit, as it was in the beginning, is now, and ever shall be, world without end. Amen.*

For further reflection

* Christ reigns in Heaven, Christ should reign on earth, and, most importantly as we make our way through Lent, Christ must reign where?

* Why do you think Pilate had his message written in three languages?

SATURDAY IN THE FIFTH WEEK OF LENT
"I thirst"

Eleventh Station: Jesus Is Nailed to the Cross

Antiphon

℣. *Adoramus Te, Christe,*	℣. *We adore You, O Christ,*
et benedicimus Tibi,	*and we praise You,*
℟. *Quia per sanctam Crucem*	℟. *Because by Your holy Cross*
Tuam redemisti mundum.	*You have redeemed the world.*

Jesus is violently thrown down on the Cross. His hands and feet are nailed to it in the most cruel way, while Jesus remains silent (St. Francis of Assisi).

John 19:28–29

After this Jesus, knowing that all was now finished, said (to fulfil the scripture), "I thirst." A bowl full of vinegar stood there; so they put a sponge full of the vinegar on hyssop and held it to his mouth.

Meditation

When else have we seen Christ thirsty? We must think back to the dusty day He sat down near Jacob's well after days of preaching, baptizing, and traveling (see John 4:5–26). He was thirsty, of course, and He asked the Samaritan woman for a drink. But more than He longed for water, He thirsted for her faith (St. Augustine).

So when we hear Christ on the Cross crying, "I thirst," we can know that again, although His thirst for water must be extreme, His thirst for the faith of the people looking up at Him is even more painful (St. Augustine). The Samaritan woman at the well gave Him the water of her faith, but what do most of the onlookers at Calvary give Him? Vinegar. Whatever good was in them has soured, just as good wine in a cracked vessel sours. They have no water of faith to offer—only the vinegar of faithlessness.

Our Lord thirsts for souls (St. Teresa of Calcutta). It makes a difference to understand His desire for souls as a *thirst*. You know that when you are extremely thirsty, it is very difficult to think of anything else. Nothing else in the world seems able to take away the fact that you desperately need water. Christ's desire for souls is like that. It is demanding. It is persistent. It won't stop until it is satisfied.

This is how much Jesus wants you to love Him with all your heart, soul, mind, and strength (see Mark 12:30). He thirsts for you.

Prayer

> O Jesus, I give myself to You entirely. Nail my heart to the Cross, that it may always remain there to love You and never leave You again (St. Alphonsus Liguori).

> Gloria Patri, et Filio, et Spiritui Sancto, sicut erat in principio, et nunc, et semper, et in saecula saeculorum. Amen.

> Glory be to the Father, and to the Son, and to the Holy Spirit, as it was in the beginning, is now, and ever shall be, world without end. Amen.

For further reflection

* How can you help satisfy Christ's thirst for souls?

* Consider Christ's love for you and His desire for you to be with Him in Heaven as a deep thirst that nothing else but your sanctification can satisfy.

XII

Jesus Dies
on the Cross

It is finished

PALM SUNDAY
The death of Our Lord

Twelfth Station: Jesus Dies on the Cross

Antiphon

℣. *Adoramus Te, Christe,*
et benedicimus Tibi,
℟. *Quia per sanctam Crucem*
Tuam redemisti mundum.

℣. *We adore You, O Christ,*
and we praise You,
℟. *Because by Your holy Cross*
You have redeemed the world.

After three hours of agony on the Cross, Jesus is finally overwhelmed with suffering and, abandoning Himself to the weight of His body, bows His head and dies (St. Alphonsus Liguori).

Luke 23:44-46
It was now about the sixth hour, and there was darkness over the whole land until the ninth hour, while the sun's light failed; and the curtain of the temple was torn in two. Then Jesus, crying with a loud voice, said, "Father, into thy hands I commit my spirit!" And having said this he breathed his last.

Meditation
In the heart of the day, all becomes dark. For three hours, the light of the sun is hidden. It is as if the darkness in the souls of men—the darkness Jesus came to earth to conquer—has been magnified to envelop the sky. If God is dying on the Cross, how can light remain? His "life was the light of men" (John 1:4).

Mysteriously, the veil of the temple is torn in two. Before, the temple veil hid the mysteries of God from the people. That was needed under the Old Covenant. But this changes with the coming of Jesus and His work on earth. Because of Christ's death, the shadowy veil that separated us from

God is torn in two. We can no longer be separated from Him, except by our own choice. People can see the mysteries of the faith with enlightened hearts and minds (St. Ambrose).

It must have come as a shock to the soldiers and the crowd when Our Lord announced the completion of His mission and His union with His Father "with a loud voice." Men who were crucified hardly had breath to speak, let alone raise their voices. Christ's supreme effort here was intentional. He would announce the end not with shame, not in defeat, but loudly (St. Ambrose). It wasn't the cry of someone giving up; it was the cry of someone proclaiming a great truth.

Now it is our turn to cry out with a loud voice. Christ's great mission is accomplished!

Prayer

> O Jesus, help me by Your grace to avoid temptation and all occasions of sin, to turn away at once from the voice of the evil one, to be regular in my prayers, and so to die to sin that You may not have died for me on the Cross in vain (St. John Henry Newman).

Gloria Patri, et Filio, et Spiritui Sancto, sicut erat in principio, et nunc, et semper, et in saecula saeculorum. Amen.	Glory be to the Father, and to the Son, and to the Holy Spirit, as it was in the beginning, is now, and ever shall be, world without end. Amen.

For further reflection

+ Then "he breathed his last." St. Luke chooses his words here carefully. He does not report that Christ lost his life. He doesn't say He gave up His life. What might the evangelist be trying to communicate?

+ Compline, or Night Prayer, in the Liturgy of the Hours always includes the responsory "Into thy hands I commend my spirit." Why do you think this is so?

MONDAY OF HOLY WEEK
"It is finished"

Twelfth Station: Jesus Dies on the Cross

Antiphon

℣. *Adoramus Te, Christe,*
et benedicimus Tibi,
℞. *Quia per sanctam Crucem*
Tuam redemisti mundum.

℣. *We adore You, O Christ,*
and we praise You,
℞. *Because by Your holy Cross*
You have redeemed the world.

Jesus hangs for three hours. During this time, He prays for His murderers, promises Paradise to the repentant robber, and commits His Blessed Mother to the care of St. John. Then all is finished, and He bows His head and gives up His spirit (St. John Henry Newman).

John 19:30
When Jesus had received the vinegar, he said, "It is finished"; and he bowed his head and gave up his spirit.

Meditation
Jesus signaled that His mission was fulfilled when He said, "It is finished." For those who were not His followers, how strange that must have sounded. What is finished? His life? One does not usually speak that way of one's own life. But Christ's work—not just the three years of His public life but His life's work as a man on earth—was complete; perfect; yes, finished.

And when? At the very time He chose, when He Himself dismissed His spirit like a master dismissing a servant with a word (Tertullian). He shed life as a man sheds a coat, at just the moment he wishes to do so (St. Augustine).

What power must be in Our Lord, if we see such power as this in Him as He dies (St. Augustine)! It is a glimmer here, in the final moments of His life, of One who, in dying, is conquering death.

"He did not wait for death, which was lagging behind ... [afraid] to come to him. Instead, he pursued it from behind and drove it on and trampled it under his feet as it was fleeing" (Eusebius of Caesarea).

Unlike Christ, we don't choose the moment we breathe our last, so we must be vigilant: always working toward the perfection and completion that His death showed us.

It is finished. Yet it is just beginning. Let us follow!

Prayer

> *O Jesus, help me by Your grace to avoid temptation and all occasions of sin, to turn away at once from the voice of the evil one, to be regular in my prayers, and so to die to sin that You may not have died for me on the Cross in vain* (St. John Henry Newman).

Gloria Patri, et Filio, et Spiritui Sancto, sicut erat in principio, et nunc, et semper, et in saecula saeculorum. Amen.	*Glory be to the Father, and to the Son, and to the Holy Spirit, as it was in the beginning, is now, and ever shall be, world without end. Amen.*

For further reflection

* Why is death not something we must fear?

* The prayer of St. John Henry Newman above indicates that prayer is an essential means of avoiding sin. Consider the connection between prayerfulness and holiness.

TUESDAY OF HOLY WEEK
Forsaken

Twelfth Station: Jesus Dies on the Cross

It is close to three o'clock, and all light is extinguished. The earth is left in darkness, and Our Lord exclaims, "It is finished!" and breathes His last (St. Josemaría Escrivá).

Mark 15:33–34

And when the sixth hour had come, there was darkness over the whole land until the ninth hour. And at the ninth hour Jesus cried with a loud voice, "Eloi, Eloi, lama sabachthani?" which means, "My God, my God, why hast thou forsaken me?"

Meditation

Christ's words in this passage are disconcerting. Our Lord is asking why the Father has abandoned Him. It is very difficult, we feel, to make sense of this.

Was this just a fancy way of expressing humility and obedience? Was it simply a way for Christ to show His acceptance of the Father's will? Not according to the Church Fathers (Origen, St. Jerome).

Instead, Christ's words testify to how completely He has "emptied himself, taking the form of a servant" (Phil. 2:7). He truly was forsaken—but He willed to be so. In fact, being forsaken by the Father was a necessary fulfillment of a mission that included taking on the sin of man, taking on death itself (Origen).

To the end, He bears witness to the Scriptures, just as He always had. He says here the first words of Psalm 22. This is a way to direct His listeners—at least those with open hearts—to the whole psalm. It is just as if I said to you, "Whose woods these are I think I know." I would want you to think of Robert Frost's whole poem. I'd be nudging you to consider how lovely silence and peace can be.

Psalm 22 begins, as you can tell, with the sufferings of a righteous man—sufferings that are prophetically similar to those of Our Lord. But just as being forsaken, "scorned by men, and despised by the people" (Ps. 22:6), is not the end of the story for Christ, it's not the end of the story in this psalm. No, the psalm ends in triumph.

Our task is to see that end ourselves, when our sufferings make us feel forsaken.

Prayer

> *O Jesus, help me by Your grace to avoid temptation and all occasions of sin, to turn away at once from the voice of the evil one, to be regular in my prayers, and so to die to sin that You may not have died for me on the Cross in vain* (St. John Henry Newman).

Gloria Patri, et Filio, et Spiritui Sancto, sicut erat in principio, et nunc, et semper, et in saecula saeculorum. Amen.	*Glory be to the Father, and to the Son, and to the Holy Spirit, as it was in the beginning, is now, and ever shall be, world without end. Amen.*

For further reflection

+ Imagine Our Lady's grief on hearing this heartrending cry of Our Lord.

+ Consider this saying of St. Gemma Galgani, who was extraordinarily devoted to the Passion of Our Lord: "If you really want to love Jesus, first learn to suffer, because suffering teaches you to love."

XIII

The Body of Jesus
Is Taken Down
from the Cross

Total gift

SPY WEDNESDAY

"Truly this was the Son of God"

Thirteenth Station: The Body of Jesus Is Taken Down from the Cross

Antiphon

℣. *Adoramus Te, Christe,*
et benedicimus Tibi,
℟. *Quia per sanctam Crucem*
Tuam redemisti mundum.

℣. *We adore You, O Christ,*
and we praise You,
℟. *Because by Your holy Cross*
You have redeemed the world.

After Our Lord has died, He is taken down from the Cross by two of His disciples, Joseph and Nicodemus, and placed in the arms of His sorrowful Mother (St. Alphonsus Liguori).

Matthew 27:54

When the centurion and those who were with him, keeping watch over Jesus, saw the earthquake and what took place, they were filled with awe, and said, "Truly this was the Son of God!"

Meditation

The centurion has been converted to faith in Christ. Our Lord had promised, "And I, when I am lifted up from the earth, will draw all men to myself" (John 12:32). Now, here on Calvary, we see this beginning to happen. The centurion is the first of all those Our Lord will draw to Himself from the Cross.

Notice, we're not just talking about any onlooker here. This is a centurion, a man who had a primary role in the torment and death of Jesus. He was respected and obeyed, and he was used to seeing men die on crosses.

Yet he observed Christ in His final hours. The man on the Cross had meekly carried His burden to Calvary; He had spoken tenderly to His Mother; He had comforted a thief; and Pilate didn't even seem to think the man had committed a crime! Even creation itself made an argument for Jesus' extraordinary nature. The centurion was moved to conclude that this was no ordinary death, no ordinary man.

The centurion stands for each of us. We, too, have a primary role in the death of Jesus because it was for our sins that He died. We see that creation testifies to His power and glory. And we have Christ's entire life to examine in the historical accounts of the Gospels. The centurion's knowledge was limited; ours is vast.

Tradition tells us that this centurion became a follower of Christ and, in time, a saint. He was deeply influenced by what he saw on Calvary. When you are at Calvary—at Mass—remember this centurion. You who have the privilege of seeing Christ's sacrifice re-presented to the Father: How will you now live differently?

Prayer

> *O Jesus crucified! I beg You: help me do what is right, and never let me be separated from your Cross. Create in me a clean heart, O Lord, that I may worthily receive You in Holy Communion and that You may remain in me, and I in You, for all eternity* (St. Francis of Assisi).

Gloria Patri, et Filio, et Spiritui Sancto, sicut erat in principio, et nunc, et semper, et in saecula saeculorum. Amen.	*Glory be to the Father, and to the Son, and to the Holy Spirit, as it was in the beginning, is now, and ever shall be, world without end. Amen.*

For further reflection

+ Judas had three years to get to know Our Lord; the centurion had only one day. What can account for the difference in their responses to Him?

+ Find out more about St. Longinus, the soldier who pierced Christ's side and was converted.

HOLY THURSDAY
Jesus knew His path would lead to the Cross

Thirteenth Station: The Body of Jesus Is Taken Down from the Cross

Antiphon

℣. *Adoramus Te, Christe,*
et benedicimus Tibi,
℟. *Quia per sanctam Crucem*
Tuam redemisti mundum.

℣. *We adore You, O Christ,*
and we praise You,
℟. *Because by Your holy Cross*
You have redeemed the world.

The crowd has gone home, and Calvary is left solitary and still, except for St. John and the holy women. Then come Joseph of Arimathea and Nicodemus, who take down from the Cross the body of Jesus, placing it in the arms of Our Lady (St. John Henry Newman).

John 6:48, 51, 53–57

I am the bread of life.... If any one eats of this bread, he will live for ever; and the bread which I shall give for the life of the world is my flesh.... Truly, truly, I say to you, unless you eat the flesh of the Son of man and drink his blood, you have no life in you; he who eats my flesh and drinks my blood has eternal life, and I will raise him up at the last day. For my flesh is food indeed, and my blood is drink indeed. He who eats my flesh and drinks my blood abides in me, and I in him. As the living Father sent me, and I live because of the Father, so he who eats me will live because of me.

Meditation

St. John records this well-loved teaching of Christ on the Holy Eucharist early in his Gospel. Do you notice that, even here, Our Lord already sees His death on the horizon? For, as He speaks, He frequently separates two things that are normally found together: body and blood. The blood is the life of the body; a living body is made up of flesh and blood together.

When we think of blood that is separated from the body, we naturally think of death. Wounds that threaten to drain the body of blood can be deadly. And indeed, those kinds of mortal wounds, beyond all telling, were what Christ suffered to establish the treasury of grace that is the Blessed Sacrament.

The Mass reflects both Christ's death and His words about His flesh and His blood. In the Mass, both bread and wine are consecrated. Though His body, blood, soul, and divinity are truly present in both the consecrated host and the consecrated wine, we speak of the host as the Body of Our Lord and the chalice as holding His Precious Blood. Only in death can these things be separated.

It is a dead body that is taken down from the Cross and placed in the arms of Our Lady. Totally poured out in love, Christ is truly gone from us. Yet that very body—in which blood will flow again at the moment of His Resurrection—is what we receive in Holy Communion.

May Our Lady's intercession make us worthy to hold within us the sacred Body and Blood of the Lord.

Prayer

> *O Jesus crucified! I beg You: help me do what is right, and never let me be separated from your Cross. Create in me a clean heart, O Lord, that I may worthily receive You in Holy Communion and that You may remain in me, and I in You, for all eternity* (St. Francis of Assisi).

Gloria Patri, et Filio, et Spiritui Sancto, sicut erat in principio, et nunc, et semper, et in saecula saeculorum. Amen.	*Glory be to the Father, and to the Son, and to the Holy Spirit, as it was in the beginning, is now, and ever shall be, world without end. Amen.*

For further reflection

* Why is Our Lady called the Mother of the Eucharist?

* Explain the meaning of this line in the Anima Christi (Soul of Christ) prayer: "Blood of Christ, inebriate me."

GOOD FRIDAY
There came forth blood and water

Thirteenth Station: The Body of Jesus Is Taken Down from the Cross

Antiphon

℣. *Adoramus Te, Christe,*
et benedicimus Tibi,
℟. *Quia per sanctam Crucem*
Tuam redemisti mundum.

℣. *We adore You, O Christ,*
and we praise You,
℟. *Because by Your holy Cross*
You have redeemed the world.

Mary stands by the Cross, and John is beside her. It is getting late, and the Jews press for our Lord to be removed from there. Joseph and Nicodemus take down the body of Jesus and place it in the arms of His most holy Mother. Mary's grief is renewed (St. Josemaría Escrivá).

John 19:31–34

Since it was the day of Preparation, in order to prevent the bodies from remaining on the cross on the sabbath (for that sabbath was a high day), the Jews asked Pilate that their legs might be broken, and that they might be taken away. So the soldiers came and broke the legs of the first, and of the other who had been crucified with him; but when they came to Jesus and saw that he was already dead, they did not break his legs. But one of the soldiers pierced his side with a spear, and at once there came out blood and water.

Meditation

The day of preparation was the sixth day of the week. For the Jews, this meant Friday.

When the world was created, God completed His work on the sixth day—on this day, creation reached its high point when God breathed life into Adam and created Eve from his side. On the sixth day then, creation was finished (St. Bede).

When the Hebrews wandered in the desert after God led them out of Egypt, it was on the sixth day that they would "gather double" the amount of manna He provided for them, so that on the Sabbath they could rest (see Exod. 16:22).

Now, on the sixth day, Christ's work is finished. His death on Good Friday ties His mission to that of creation. On *this* sixth day, Christ has accomplished the reconciliation of all humanity back to what it was in the beginning (St. Bede). No more separation from our Creator, no more closed gates to paradise, no more flaming sword keeping man out. It has all been overcome by One like us in all things but sin.

Christ's work is finished, and we, on this sixth day, are to "gather double." Yes, we are to partake of the abundance of graces Christ won for us. But how?

The blood and water flowing from His side show us how. Christ's death makes possible the sacramental graces of Baptism (water) and the Eucharist (blood). As Christ's side was opened with a spear, the gate of life was opened to the Church (St. Augustine).

Prayer

> *O Jesus crucified! I beg You: help me do what is right, and never let me be separated from your Cross. Create in me a clean heart, O Lord, that I may worthily receive You in Holy Communion and that You may remain in me, and I in You, for all eternity* (St. Francis of Assisi).

Gloria Patri, et Filio, et Spiritui Sancto, sicut erat in principio, et nunc, et semper, et in saecula saeculorum. Amen.	*Glory be to the Father, and to the Son, and to the Holy Spirit, as it was in the beginning, is now, and ever shall be, world without end. Amen.*

For further reflection

* Out of the side of Adam was made a bride. How can we say the same of Our Lord (St. Ephrem the Syrian)?

* How does the door Noah made in the side of the ark prefigure the "door" made by the soldier in the side of Christ?

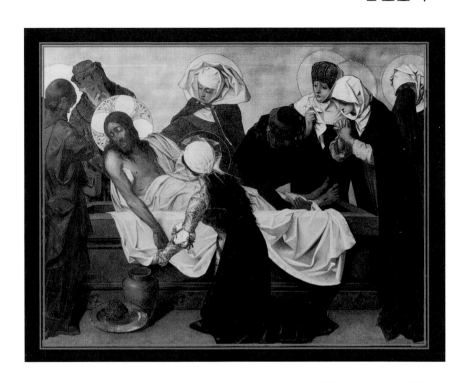

XIV

Jesus Is
Laid in the Tomb

Darkness

HOLY SATURDAY
Jesus is hastily buried

Fourteenth Station: Jesus Is Laid in the Tomb

Antiphon

℣. *Adoramus Te, Christe,*
et benedicimus Tibi,
℟. *Quia per sanctam Crucem*
Tuam redemisti mundum.

℣. *We adore You, O Christ,*
and we praise You,
℟. *Because by Your holy Cross*
You have redeemed the world.

Very near Calvary, in an orchard, Joseph of Arimathea had had a new
tomb made, cut out of the rock. Since it is the eve of the solemn Pasch of
the Jews, Jesus is laid there. Then Joseph, rolling a great stone, closes the
grave door and goes away (St. Josemaría Escrivá).

John 19:38–42

After this Joseph of Arimathea, who was a disciple of Jesus, but secretly, for
fear of the Jews, asked Pilate that he might take away the body of Jesus, and
Pilate gave him leave. So he came and took away his body. Nicodemus also,
who had at first come to him by night, came bringing a mixture of myrrh
and aloes, about a hundred pounds' weight. They took the body of Jesus,
and bound it in linen cloths with the spices, as is the burial custom of the
Jews. Now in the place where he was crucified there was a garden, and in
the garden a new tomb where no one had ever been laid. So because of the
Jewish day of Preparation, as the tomb was close at hand, they laid Jesus there.

Meditation

Jesus is laid in a beautiful new tomb, and we see the first-ever tabernacle
of Our Lord's body and blood.

The tomb has held no other dead man before this, for this dead man is
like no other (Origen). This tomb, this tabernacle, is in a garden because

in a garden man lost Paradise. He was forced out of Paradise—he had to be kept away from the tree of life so that he would not eat of it and extend his misery for all time.

But in *this* garden, Christ, the vine, is "planted" in order to root out all the thorns and thistles of sin that had taken over (St. Cyril of Jerusalem).

Although no one had been buried there before, countless people would be buried there in the future (Origen). For all the followers of Christ throughout the ages are buried with Him in Baptism, that they might rise with Him to new life (Rom. 6:4–5).

Let us watch and wait through the darkness—because a garden is not for dead things. It is where things come to life.

Prayer

> *O Jesus, lie down and sleep in peace in the calm grave for a little while, and then wake up for an everlasting reign. We, like the faithful women, will watch around You, for all our treasure, all our life, is lodged with You* (St. John Henry Newman).

Gloria Patri, et Filio, et Spiritui Sancto, sicut erat in principio, et nunc, et semper, et in saecula saeculorum. Amen.	*Glory be to the Father, and to the Son, and to the Holy Spirit, as it was in the beginning, is now, and ever shall be, world without end. Amen.*

For further reflection

- In many icons depicting Holy Saturday, Christ is shown standing on a broken gate. What is that gate?

- In the Creed, we profess that Our Lord descended into hell. What is "hell" in this context, and what did Christ do there?

XV

The Resurrection

Triumph

EASTER SUNDAY
Christ is risen!

Matthew 28:1–10
Now after the sabbath, toward the dawn of the first day of the week, Mary Magdalene and the other Mary went to see the sepulchre. And behold, there was a great earthquake; for an angel of the Lord descended from heaven and came and rolled back the stone, and sat upon it. His appearance was like lightning, and his raiment white as snow. And for fear of him the guards trembled and became like dead men. But the angel said to the women, "Do not be afraid; for I know that you seek Jesus who was crucified. He is not here; for he has risen, as he said. Come, see the place where he lay. Then go quickly and tell his disciples that he has risen from the dead, and behold, he is going before you to Galilee; there you will see him. Lo, I have told you." So they departed quickly from the tomb with fear and great joy, and ran to tell his disciples. And behold, Jesus met them and said, "Hail!" And they came up and took hold of his feet and worshiped him. Then Jesus said to them, "Do not be afraid; go and tell my brethren to go to Galilee, and there they will see me."

Meditation
At the end of the Stabat Mater hymn, we ask for the grace to bear in our own bodies the death of Our Lord: to carry with us always His suffering, His Passion, His death.

Even today, on Easter, we remember the sufferings of Our Lord. We do not forget the Cross because we know that God does not forget the Cross. If the Cross was to be forgotten, Our Lord would not have appeared to the apostle Thomas with the marks of the nails and the spear in His hands, feet, and side. He would not be shown to us as a "lamb who was slain" (see Rev. 5:6). In Heaven, He bears these five marks of what He suffered for us.

We live as followers of the Risen Lord. But as we carry that joy always in our hearts, we know that we are to bear His Cross too. There is no separating one mission from the other, just as there is no separation of the Cross and the Resurrection in Our Lord. The triumph could not have come about without the trial.

"The life of man upon earth is a warfare" (Job 7:1, Douay-Rheims): we are soldiers. But we're different from most soldiers because we know exactly how to win. In fact, we know that our Commander has already won. So let us soldier on: "Do not be afraid!" *O Lord, let Your Cross be my victory! Christ is risen! Alleluia!*

Prayer

℣. *Regina caeli, laetare, alleluia.*
℟. *Quia quem meruisti portare, alleluia.*
℣. *Resurrexit, sicut dixit, alleluia.*
℟. *Ora pro nobis Deum, alleluia.*
℣. *Gaude et laetare, Virgo Maria, alleluia.*
℟. *Quia surrexit Dominus vere, alleluia.*
Oremus. Deus, qui per resurrectionem Filii tui, Domini nostri Iesu Christi, mundum laetificare dignatus es: praesta, quaesumus; ut per eius Genetricem Virginem Mariam, perpetuae capiamus gaudia vitae. Per eundem Christum Dominum nostrum. Amen.

℣. *Queen of Heaven, rejoice, alleluia.*
℟. *For He whom you did merit to bear, alleluia.*
℣. *Has risen, as He said, alleluia.*
℟. *Pray for us to God, alleluia.*
℣. *Rejoice and be glad, O Virgin Mary, alleluia.*
℟. *For the Lord has truly risen, alleluia.*
Let us pray. O God, who gave joy to the world through the Resurrection of Thy Son, Our Lord Jesus Christ, grant we beseech Thee, that through the intercession of the Virgin Mary, His Mother, we may obtain the joys of everlasting life. Through the same Christ our Lord. Amen.

For further reflection

* If you are not familiar with the Regina Caeli chant, listen to a recording of it.

* Study the text of the eleventh-century Easter sequence, Victimae Paschali Laudes (Praises to the Paschal Victim), and listen to a sung recording of it:

Victimae Paschali Laudes

Víctimae Pascháli laudes immolent Christiáni.	Let Christians sacrifice praise To the Paschal Victim.
Agnus redémit oves: Christus ínnocens Patri reconciliávit peccatóres.	The Lamb has redeemed the sheep! Christ, who is innocent, has reconciled sinners to the Father.
Mors et vita duello conflixére mirando: Dux vitae mórtuus regnat vivus.	Death and Life clashed In a spectacular battle: The Commander of life, having died, reigns alive.
Dic nobis María, quid vidisti in via?	Tell us, Mary, what did you see on the way?
"Sepulcrum Christi viventis, et gloriam vidi resurgentis: Angélicos testes, sudarium, et vestes.	"I saw the tomb of Christ and the glory of His rising, angelic witnesses, the head napkin, and the linen cloths.
Surrexit Christus spes mea: praecédet suos in Galilaeam."	Christ my Hope is risen! He will go before His own into Galilee."
Scimus Christum surrexisse a mórtuis vere:	We know that Christ is truly risen from the dead:
Tu nobis, victor Rex, miserére. Amen. Allelúja.	O Christ the Victor, have mercy on us. Amen. Alleluia.

Stabat Mater

Literally translated, the title of this traditional Lenten hymn, used particularly with the Stations of the Cross, is "The mother was standing." Our Lady walked the Way of the Cross along with her Son and then *was standing*, for three hours, keeping watch over His agony.

Stabat Mater dolorosa
iuxta Crucem lacrimosa,
dum pendebat Filius.

Cuius animam gementem,
contristatam et dolentem
pertransivit gladius.

O quam tristis et afflicta
fuit illa benedicta,
mater Unigeniti!

Quae maerebat et dolebat,
pia Mater, dum videbat
nati poenas inclyti.

Quis est homo qui non fleret,
matrem Christi si videret
in tanto supplicio?

At the Cross her station keeping,
stood the mournful Mother weeping,
close to Jesus to the last.

Through her heart, His sorrow sharing,
all His bitter anguish bearing,
now at length the sword has passed.

O how sad and sore distressed
was that Mother, highly blest,
of the sole-begotten One.

Christ above in torment hangs,
she beneath beholds the pangs
of her dying glorious Son.

Is there one who would not weep,
whelmed in miseries so deep,
Christ's dear Mother to behold?

Quis non posset contristari
Christi Matrem contemplari
dolentem cum Filio?

Pro peccatis suae gentis
vidit Iesum in tormentis,
et flagellis subditum.

Vidit suum dulcem Natum
moriendo desolatum,
dum emisit spiritum.

Eia, Mater, fons amoris
me sentire vim doloris
fac, ut tecum lugeam.

Fac, ut ardeat cor meum
in amando Christum Deum
ut sibi complaceam.

Sancta Mater, istud agas,
crucifixi fige plagas
cordi meo valide.

Tui Nati vulnerati,
tam dignati pro me pati,
poenas mecum divide.

Fac me tecum pie flere,
crucifixo condolere,
donec ego vixero.

Iuxta Crucem tecum stare,
et me tibi sociare
in planctu desidero.

Can the human heart refrain
from partaking in her pain,
in that Mother's pain untold?

Bruised, derided, cursed, defiled,
she beheld her tender Child
All with bloody scourges rent:

For the sins of His own nation,
saw Him hang in desolation,
Till His spirit forth He sent.

O thou Mother! fount of love!
Touch my spirit from above,
make my heart with thine accord:

Make me feel as thou hast felt;
make my soul to glow and melt
with the love of Christ my Lord.

Holy Mother! pierce me through,
in my heart each wound renew
of my Savior crucified:

Let me share with thee His pain,
who for all my sins was slain,
who for me in torments died.

Let me mingle tears with thee,
mourning Him who mourned for me,
all the days that I may live:

By the Cross with thee to stay,
there with thee to weep and pray,
is all I ask of thee to give.

Virgo virginum praeclara,
mihi iam non sis amara,
fac me tecum plangere.

Fac, ut portem Christi mortem,
passionis fac consortem,
et plagas recolere.

Fac me plagis vulnerari,
fac me Cruce inebriari,
et cruore Filii.

Flammis ne urar succensus,
per te, Virgo, sim defensus
in die iudicii.

Christe, cum sit hinc exire,
da per Matrem me venire
ad palmam victoriae.

Quando corpus morietur,
fac, ut animae donetur
paradisi gloria. Amen.

Virgin of all virgins blest!,
Listen to my fond request:
let me share thy grief divine:

Let me, to my latest breath,
in my body bear the death
of that dying Son of thine.

Wounded with His every wound,
steep my soul till it hath swooned,
in His very Blood away:

Be to me, O Virgin, nigh,
lest in flames I burn and die,
in His awful Judgment Day.

Christ, when Thou shalt call me hence,
be Thy Mother my defense,
be Thy Cross my victory;

While my body here decays,
may my soul Thy goodness praise,
safe in paradise with Thee. Amen.

About the Author

Suzan Sammons is a mother of seven children and young adults and the author of *The Jesse Tree: An Advent Devotion.* Her involvement in the prolife movement over three decades included sidewalk counseling at abortion centers and running a nonprofit adoption foundation. She is a homeschooling mother and editor of several Catholic publications, and she has published numerous articles in Catholic outlets on topics including child-rearing and education, the dignity of the unborn, holistic health, and Catholic spirituality.

Sophia Institute

Sophia Institute is a nonprofit institution that seeks to nurture the spiritual, moral, and cultural life of souls and to spread the gospel of Christ in conformity with the authentic teachings of the Roman Catholic Church.

Sophia Institute Press fulfills this mission by offering translations, reprints, and new publications that afford readers a rich source of the enduring wisdom of mankind.

Sophia Institute also operates the popular online resource CatholicExchange.com. *Catholic Exchange* provides world news from a Catholic perspective as well as daily devotionals and articles that will help readers to grow in holiness and live a life consistent with the teachings of the Church.

In 2013, Sophia Institute launched Sophia Institute for Teachers to renew and rebuild Catholic culture through service to Catholic education. With the goal of nurturing the spiritual, moral, and cultural life of souls, and an abiding respect for the role and work of teachers, we strive to provide materials and programs that are at once enlightening to the mind and ennobling to the heart; faithful and complete, as well as useful and practical.

Sophia Institute gratefully recognizes the Solidarity Association for preserving and encouraging the growth of our apostolate over the course of many years. Without their generous and timely support, this book would not be in your hands.

www.SophiaInstitute.com
www.CatholicExchange.com
www.SophiaInstituteforTeachers.org

Sophia Institute Press® is a registered trademark of Sophia Institute.
Sophia Institute is a tax-exempt institution as defined by the
Internal Revenue Code, Section 501(c)(3). Tax ID 22-2548708.